Horses Know The Way Home

Inspirational Whisperings

The Collection

Vol. 1

Brian Reid

Text copyright © 2013 Brian Reid

All rights reserved. No part of this book may be reproduced or transmitted in any form or by any means, electronic or mechanical, including photocopying, recording or by an information storage and retrieval system. A reviewer may quote brief passages in a review to be printed in a magazine or newspaper with permission in writing from the publisher. For information, contact LSI Inc., Horses Know The Way Home: info@horsesknowthewayhome.com

www.HorsesKnowTheWayHome.com

Photographs by: Jaimie and Jonathan Jusczyk and Tina Thuell
Cover creation by: Jennifer Stamps
Edited by: Katleen Reid

Published by: LSI Inc.

ISBN: 978-0989169103

First edition: April 2013

Special Thanks to: Cynthia Plakias, Elena Sloops-Wildes, Lorraine Dennis Ph.D.

Give Yourself a Gift

Table of Contents

Toward	**6**
Introduction	**8**
Whispering 1: Horse Whisperings	11
Whispering 2: Feel the Connection	17
Whispering 3: It's about the Journey	19
Whispering 4: Something Large, Something New	23
Whispering 5: Great-itude	27
Whispering 6: Happiness Hunting	31
Whispering 7: Rut-Row to Let's Go!	35
Whispering 8: Great Answers Begin with Great Answers	39
Whispering 9: Imagine a Feeling	43
Whispering 10: Release the Jaw	47
The Space of Innocence	**51**
Whispering 11: Put the Cart Before the Horse	53
Whispering 12: Claiming Your Personal Horsepower!	57
Whispering 13: Online and 5 bars strong	61
Whispering 14: Goal Setting Wi-Fi	65
Whispering 15: Fall in Love with Your Life	69
Whispering 16: Awe, Are, Ahhhhh ...	73
Whispering 17: Balancing your heart with your mind begins with your Butt	77
Whispering 18: You Are Enough	81
Whispering 19: The Rhythms of Life	85
Whispering 20: To Be or not To Be?	89
Look for the Gaps in Life	**93**
Whispering 21: 3 Steps to a Great A-Game	95
Whispering 22: It's About What it Becomes	99
Whispering 23: Small Releases Set Us Free	103
Whispering 24: Blame, Blame, Go Away	107
Whispering 25: JBT, the Miracle Drug	111
Whispering 26: Smile with all four cheeks	115
Whispering 27: Let Go ... Gone ... Going	119
Whispering 28: The Bubble	123
Whispering 29: Pick the Pattern that Pleases	127
Whispering 30: Balancing the Forces of Nature to Create Momentum in Your Life	131
Let's Play Today!	**135**

Whispering 31: We Are Feeling Beings	137
Whispering 32: Follow your Light	141
Whispering 33: Powerful Vibrations	145
Whispering 34: Get your Freque on!	147
Whispering 35: Respect Yourself	149
Whispering 36: There is Life after Death	153
Whispering 37: A Powerful and Pleasing Journey	157
Whispering 38: To Ponder or to Wonder	161
Whispering 39: Find your Weeeeeeeeeeee!!!	163
Whispering 40: Close Your Eyes and See the Light	169

The Rhythms of our Lives — 173

Whispering 41: Are you Dancing?	175
Whispering 42: The True Expression of Gratitude, Grace and Next!	181
Whispering 43: Following my Desire to Heaven on Earth	187
Whispering 44: Follow your Heart	193
Whispering 45: Winning the Race of Life, Right Now!	195
Whispering 46: How do you experience others?	199
Whispering 47: Fulfilling Freedom of Witnessing a Flying Shire	201
Whispering 48: Patterns that Serve	207
Whispering 49: The Art of Let's Go	211
Whispering 50: You are listening to HKTWH FM radio!	215
Whispering 51: Smile While you Walk	219
Whispering 52: Let What Matters Become Matter!	223

Just Breathe — 227

Bonus Whisperings

1: Beating the "Blah's"	229
2: Our Rented Planet, Your Gifted Time	235

Photographs by — 240

Jaimie and Jonathan Jusczyk	240
Tina Thuell	241

About Brian Reid and Horses Know The Way Home — 242

Toward

Toward what you might ask?
Toward what Inspirational Whisperings are calling us.

Toward home!

All my life, through all the trials and tribulations, through all the triumphs and celebrations, there were always two presences, two consciousnesses watching me as I lived my life.

One witness was always analyzing, judging, evaluating and measuring everything I did. This awareness changed from moment to moment and situation to situation and transformed as the years went by. One moment this judger of my life was my biggest fan, the next my biggest critic. I always tried to measure up to its constant judgment, only to get lost in the "less than, more than" rollercoaster of its ever changing perspectives and interpretations. It is and was exhausting.

The other presence has been with me, watching in whispered silence from day one. Never judging, always loving, constantly calling me toward what matters most to me deep inside.

This accepting, loving, presence always speaks in gentle whispers, that when listened to, thunders the truth of my being and always beckoned toward my becoming.

It was only when I came to spend time in the presence of Brenda Lee, the Shire mare I've shared my life with for the last 15 years, that the whisperings became a clear, consistent and commanding voice that I leaned toward to direct my actions. This constant leaning has become a *momenting* energy that pulls me toward the imagined life of my dreams.

While Brenda Lee's immense size, sheer power, and physical beauty mesmerizes my mind, her silent, accepting awareness melts my heart with the essence of unconditional love.

It is in this space, where the drama of my life's thoughts and story holds no ground, that I begin to hear the *Inspirational Whisperings* that have changed my life forever and make sense of the timeless truths that poets and sages have passed down through the ages.

That Awareness, Acceptance and Love, *matter* and that Forgiveness, Gratitude and Appreciation are *verbs* to be acted out in order to discover what we have known inside all along.

We are enough!
We matter!
What we Love, matters!

It is from this place, where thoughts come through me but not from me, that these Inspirational Whisperings have come; always in the presence of Brenda Lee, always in response to a heartfelt asking.

It is my deep desire that while reading these Inspirational Whisperings, you are moved to act on your own Whispered Inspirations, calling you toward your perfect becoming, calling you home.

Feel the Connection
Brian Reid

P.S. Lucy, Eddie and Red Dog wish to say they like hanging out while Whisperings are being listened to.

Introduction

What is Horses Know The Way Home?

Horses Know The Way Home (HKTWH) is an international personal development company that uses the model of *the horse* to exemplify the natural laws we all live by in a unique, interactive and playful way.

Brian Reid (creator of HKTWH) and his Shire mare Brenda Lee help you feel the connection to your inner truth (IT) from where you can express, create and move forward in life toward what matters to you. Through *feeling the connection* between Brian, Brenda Lee and the dogs – Lucy, Eddie and Red Dog - you will start to feel the beautiful dynamics life has to offer that are within your own reach.

The HKTWH Whisperings are a part of the HKTWH Academy. Through sharing his adventures with Brenda Lee in Whisperings, Brian sheds a light on how Brenda Lee teaches him the 13 HKTWH Academy Principles and how he applies them into his own life.

And so can you!

Lucy, Brian and Brenda Lee *Eddie, Lucy, Brian and Red Dog ... and Brenda Lee*

At Horses Know The Way Home, the horse is the teacher, the humans are the students and the subject is the game of life!

Are you ready to play?

Let's Go ... !

© Tina Thuell

Whispering 1

Horse Whisperings

Pssst! Psssst!!!
Come closer.
I have secrets I want to tell you.

Ssshhh! SSSHHHH!!!
Someone will hear you.
Keep your voice down.
Bring your ear closer.

I have some secrets I need to *whisper* to you.
Secrets that will set you FREE.
Free to be the person you know you are inside.
Free to release the doubts that you are not worthy, that I feel you holding onto.

Ssshhhh!!!
Someone is coming.
Close your eyes and act like you are sleeping.

These secrets can only be heard by those who are ready.
So we want to be particular about whom we share them with.
The most important thing is that you hear them for yourself.
Don't worry if you don't understand them all right away.
You will GET the ones you are ready to hear.
Those that you are not yet ready for will hang in your closet.

Like a nice warm sweater waiting for that cool day when you need it.
On that day it will FEEL warm and comforting.

And you'll be glad that you have it.

These secrets have many layers to them.
So I will only share with you
What you can use and handle right now:

The first secret is

You use three forms of communication

1. Words
2. Tone of Voice
3. Body Language

to convey who you are
and what you want
to yourself and others.

Words don't communicate the truth as effectively as you think.
Neither does tone of voice.
Body Language is the most effective form of communication for:

1. Telling the truth about your current situation and
2. Determining if what you are doing is working for you.

In other words; if **IT** feels right, **IT** is…
and if **IT** doesn't, **IT** isn't.
IT is your *Inner Truth* and **IT** is always speaking to you through your body.

Can you feel **IT**?
Haven't you always felt **IT**?

You know! "Women's intuition".
Or, for the men it can be called a "Gut feeling".

Ssshhh!
Behind you!
Someone's listening

Smile, act natural.

There are forces that would keep these secrets from you.
So that you would have to look for them to know who you are.
I tell you that everyone has access to them and they are free to all,
If you will just open up your heart
And listen to your feelings.

The reason I can tell you these secrets is because:
As a Horse I don't have concerns of the past,
Worries of the future,
Or the drama of my "life story" swirling in my mind,
Blocking me from my awareness of "What Is".

I'm always connected to **IT**.

So, back to Body Language:
If you listen to your feelings
Choose thoughts that make you feel better.
Assume a state of being or body position that is in line with what you want.
In other words, "Say it with the physical attitude that you would have
If you had already received what you want".
Then, riches in line with your imagination and desires await you!

One last thing:
Since these "Secrets" are available to everyone,
They aren't really secrets, are they?

Between you and me, let's call them **"Whisperings"**
Because I can't speak your language
You will have to listen really, really carefully to mine in order to hear them.

"Whisperings" are like the wind through the trees.

The rustling of the leaves.

The silence between words.

They are always there, you just have to lean in their direction and allow them in.

If anyone asks you
Where you heard these Whisperings,
Say you heard it right from the horse's mouth!
Right here!
Right now!

In the moment.
The only place and time that exists...
The only place I live.

Brenda Lee

© Tina Thuell

Whispering 2
Feel the Connection

I like to say **"Feel the Connection"** a lot.
Sometimes, I find that I may be over-thinking too much. But I don't do this often or for too long. Whenever I get to the root of each personal development principle I'm contemplating or practicing,
I realize it is all about **The Connection**.

The connection with ourselves and our life story.
The connection with others and their life story.

When I spend time with Brenda Lee, Lucy, Eddie and Red walking together, or we experience the sheer joy of just playing, I realize there is another connection. One that has no story. One that simply exists and always exists. And I am simply reminded of it's existence.

It exists in the here and now.
It connects me with who I am at that moment.
It connects me with others.
It connects me with that which connects us all.

Or, should I say, I'm reminded of that which we are all connected to? It is always there. We only need to feel it, or feel for it. It will feel back for you if you are open to it - just by witnessing others feeling it.

Can you see Lucy connecting with Brenda? Can you **Feel the Connection**?
There is something out there, and in here, that we connect with. And when I have felt it, I know in my bones that what I'm connecting to is all that matters. I am grateful for the beings and entities in my life that remind me of this feeling when I experience them.

They remind me that **Feeling the Connection** is my work and my play. It is my reason for living.

Do you feel it?

Feel the Connection

© Jonathan Jusczyk

Whispering 3

It's about the Journey

"The proper preparation starts with a goal that means something to you. Let go of things that are holding you back. Then take the first step toward what feels good with a smile on your face and don't look back."

You mark the progression of your life through a series of achievements- whether those markers are the passing of birthdays, graduations, new jobs, weddings, new houses and big moves, big promotions or new offices- when you tell the tales of your life to someone else you always mark the passage of time as "before I married..." or, "after I got the promotion...." or, "when we moved here...."

Goals ARE life. And the upward battle to grasp onto the next one and wrestle it into your pocket is a *lot* of work - until you make the proper preparations.

It's never about the goal itself, large or small.
It's about the journey there.

Have you ever looked back at an achievement, at the hours you spent getting there, and suddenly realized that it wasn't as bad as you thought it would be? Enjoying the steps to accomplishing something actually makes it that much easier for you to get there. Goals are nothing more than something you WANT in life, and it's that WANTING that inspires and drives you toward the goal. Achieving personal life goals is truly all in the prep – or, all in the moments before the achievement. Preparation can make that thing you wanted seem like it dropped into your lap without any effort at all, simply because you were enjoying the journey there so much.

LET GO of the stress and the pain. You can get what you WANT by wanting it, and getting there will be nothing but enjoyment. Life is there for you to enjoy every moment- whether it's that high point of achieving that goal or every second in between.

During the filming of **Series 12: It's All in the Prep** for the HKTWH Academy, I set myself the goal to "Indian Mount" Brenda Lee. I used all of the previous 11 principles to help prepare myself for the task to leap onto Brenda Lee's back from the ground. This may not have been a huge life-changing goal, but I thought it would be a fun desire to practice my preparations with.

What is one of your goals? It doesn't matter if it will be life-changing and monumental, or simply something that would bring you joy to accomplish.

The important thing is to remember – it's all in the prep!

Feel the Connection

"When you want to find your way home, follow your bliss, Let Go toward living the life you desire; your spirit has to be in harmony with your head and heart in balance."

© Jaimie Jusczyk

Whispering 4

Something Large, Something New

Something large, something new.
Something unusual, something beautiful.
Something powerful, something cool.

This is how you discover, expand and express the ever-new you.

As I took six open hearts swimming with Brenda Lee and Lucy, I had the privilege of being the moved witness as each person experienced the large, new, unusual, beautiful, powerful and cool.

What I heard was laughter.
What I saw was joy.
What I felt was each human heart open, as it felt free to express happiness on a grand scale.
What I knew was that the intensity of this blissful state will keep moving through each life, attracting other like experiences to each person, just in its simple reflection.

When we accept ourselves as we are while allowing ourselves to become what we know we are capable of, we often still need help in moving beyond the gravitational pull of our **NOW** patterns.

The life situations that have brought us here may not serve us on the next leg of our journey.

In times like these we can "*find that feeling*" of large, new, unusual, beautiful, powerful and cool, as felt by the uniqueness that is us in any given moment. This combination of traits will open our eyes to greater depths of ourselves and fill our spirit with enough joy to pursue our glorious **NEXT**.

Something large enough that you will surrender to its inspiration.
Something new enough that your mind will be intrigued.
Something unusual enough that its "outside the box-ness" will not allow reference to the old while opening your heart to new possibilities.
Something beautiful enough that your heart will invite it in.
Something powerful enough that it will lift you over the walls of mediocrity and into possibility.
Something cool enough that it at once tickles your funny bone as well as sets fire to the wishes of others who witness.

Go forth and say, "**YES!**" to experiences that look and feel like this to you.
Go forth and create these experiences in your imagination. Then step into them with a whisper, followed by a resounding "**YES!**" as you reflect on your courage to become **YOU**.

Come home to yourself. Get comfortable in self acceptance.
Then go outside and play, it is a beautiful day!

Feel the Connection

© Jaimie Jusczyk

Whispering 5

Great-itude

The act of increasing your attitude and gratitude toward something.

Direct your thoughts and feelings to create an "attitude of gratitude" that will attract greatness to you.

How big is *great-itude*?

As big or as small as it needs to be.
Great-itude involves using your mind to consciously seek out the thoughts that will create good feelings for you. These good feelings can then be amplified into "*momenting*" energy, and this energy force will become a self-sustaining state of gratitude and love that, once established, continues replicating and reverberating itself throughout your life.

I am filled with *great-itude* every morning when I drive up the farm entry and come to the end of a hedgerow. Although I'm still about 30 yards away from Brenda Lee's stall door, I slow the car down and focus my attention to her soft pink and black nose as she peeks out toward me, awaiting my arrival. As I witness her welcoming, I always see the fluttering of her nostrils, calling me to come to her.

This clear moment of chosen connection resonates *great-itude* within me because I chose to acknowledge it, I appreciated it, I amplified it and then I let it flow into all the other aspects in my life.

It's a simple act: "fluttering nostrils", but when brought into focus with *great-itude*, Brenda Lee's fluttering nostrils become a daily meditation in the way that life can respond to me, as opposed to my responding to life.

Find the simple moments within your day - your *great-itudes*. Notice them. Appreciate them. Amplify and apply them. Even the smallest *great-itudes* practiced daily can change your life.

A few examples of my other *great-itude* triggers include:

- Brenda Lee waiting motionless in her stall opening as I place her halter on every morning before we head outside to graze.
- Lucy, waiting until I'm ready to go to sleep, and then jumping on the bed with me to snuggle in the space between my right arm and hip.
- Eddie, always and ever-silently present at my right side as we walk on the beach together.
- Red Dog sitting next to me on the couch for an entire movie - as if he's just as interested in the movie as I am!
- The steady streams of appreciation from all of the HKTWH posts on the Community blogs, forums, Facebook page, You tube videos and the Whisperings.
- Brenda Lee hearing my car approaching and running to wait for me at the gate at the end of each day.
- Noticing Brenda Lee's soft eye, then her eyelashes, then my own reflection in her eye as she receives me in her presence; then to make the same association with a friend with whom I've made a connection.

... these are all *great-itudes* that fill my life.

Increase your attitude and gratitude toward the little things in your life.
What *great-itude* awaits you today?

Feel the Connection

"To be in the presence of free beings fully expressing themselves without restriction wakes something in the depth of our being that is more valuable than gold and more precious than diamonds and free for us all if we just look for it. But you must look with the eyes of your heart.

Can you see?"

© Tina Thuell

Whispering 6

Happiness Hunting

"Outside the Box"
"Outside the Patterns of Survival" and,
"In the Land of Imagination"

We humans are an incredibly adaptive species.

On November 24, 1859 Charles Darwin published *On the Origin of Species*, a work of scientific literature which is considered to be the foundation of evolutionary biology. Its full title was *On the Origin of Species by Means of Natural Selection, or the Preservation of Favored Races in the Struggle for Life*.

Darwin is often associated with the saying "**Survival of the Fittest**".

Charles would have been fascinated by our ability to "fit in" and our ability to accommodate and blend with the struggle for life.

Our ability to adapt to incredibly life threatening situations and environments on our planet is amazing. No other vertebrate on the planet can survive in such varied climate and conditions as humans. We can be found in the frozen Arctic and Antarctic, in humid bug infested jungles, in hot arid deserts, on and in the Ocean. We can use our ingenuity to adapt by creating machines, clothing and protective man-made environments that will allow us to survive in inhospitable climates.

It is exactly this ability survive, to adapt, accommodate and "fit in" that is our biggest obstacle when it come to providing ourselves with happiness.

We can adapt to lives of addiction, abuse, poverty, and mindsets of lack as easily as the harshest of environments that the planet has to offer us.

We can survive.

The question is will we LIVE?

Will we look for, find, nurture and create happiness for ourselves?
Will we "hunt happiness" like it is our last meal?
Will we focus on creating our happiness environment like our lives depend on it?

Because of our ability to adapt, our biggest enemy to happiness is complacency. We stop, look and just settle for what is. We "fit in".

The odd thing is, the life we are fitting into at one time did not exist and someone decided to create it. Someone decided to go beyond the edge of acceptance and explore outside the box of what was currently accepted as "the norm".

Someone decided to leave the life raft and swim to the shores in search of happiness.

At *Horses Know the Way Home*, we help people look beyond and feel for a connection with something "outside the box" of the predictable patterns that can often ensnare us in mediocrity.

We offer individuals feelings of wonder, joy, happiness, beauty and power; "Outside the Box", "Outside the Patterns of Survival" and in the land of imagination.

"*Imagination is more important than Knowledge*" - Albert Einstein

This land where "anything is possible" is a land that only humans can inhabit. And we must, if we are to truly *live*. We must go to this land and hunt for our happiness like our lives depend on it.

Once our hearts have felt these experiences, our minds can go about the task of hunting them down and bringing them home to feast on.

Before you embark on your hunt for happiness, you will need to look for some very specific tools to bring along with you:

- Gratitude
- Laughter
- Joy
- Friendship
- Vulnerability
- Compassion
- Willingness
- Awareness
- Partnership
- Play

Start there, and begin your hunt (or play might be a more effective word to use) for your happiness.

Look for experiences "outside the box" of what you know and "inside the good feelings of your imagination" and start leaning toward them with all your heart.

All you need to do is say YES to the cool stuff life is offering you at the edge of what you already know.

Feel IT and Do IT!

Feel the Connection

Whispering 7

Rut-Row to Let's Go!

From the very first "Ruh-Roh George!" uttered from the muzzle of George Jetson's dog, Astro, as a warning to George in The Jetsons cartoon to Scooby's later version of "Ruh-Roh Shaggy" in Scooby Doo, we all have learned to heed the warnings in these words.

In both cartoons, we are reminded of these familiar and repetitive "Uh-Oh's!". They repeat a similar warning in each episode. And in every entertaining predicament, we watched with great anticipation to see what would happen next.

These "Ruh-Row's!" remind me of the "RUT-ROWS" we get ourselves into. We stay in them day-in and day-out, week-in and week-out…on and on until the list of our personal re-run episodes can seem longer than all of The Jetsons and Scooby Doo cartoons combined.

"RUT-ROWS" - the proverbial ruts (or ingrained behavioral patterns) in which we can get stuck. Our patterns have us stuck within a repetition creating such depth that eventually we cannot even seem to see any other options beyond it - because we have bogged ourselves down too deeply into the rut. The banks loom high above our heads and obscure the view of any other alternative. You can become ensnared by the rut which you have created with repetitive patterns that are no longer working for you.

Can you identify the RUT-ROWS that are holding you back?
Are there areas of your life that look and feel like, "Here I go again… I've already been here and done this"?

Work, relationships, family, personal care, dreams and imagination can all suffer when we go back and forth only within the rows we have created. They suffer when you are living in the ruts of patterns that no longer serve you and you are no longer moving toward what you now desire.

How can you get out of this "RUT-ROW" mentality and move into your "Let's Go!" reality?

Start with your imagination: set it free, and imagine a life or a situation that brings a smile to your face, warmth to your heart and a tingle to your skin. Imagine something unusual beyond the usual "RUT-ROW!" response.
This will take a focused and relaxed effort. With a cleansing breath, allow love to flow into every fiber of your being. Imagine a life that excites you. You will need this powerful mindset to get beyond the banks of the ruts that currently imprison you.

While you hold that new and positive image, allow yourself to nurture that feeling. Next, magnify it and start leaning toward what feels better to you.
Look around your life for all examples of anything that you feel grateful for. Look for what you love. Resonate with love and feel yourself being lifted out of your current reality and moving toward your imagined NEXT and your Let's Go!

Are you able to do this?
Try it, and notice how the miraculous becomes normal.
Do this until you start to expect miracles.

People always ask me what it is that we do at Horses Know the Way Home.
There is no brief answer, but the secret that I give to them is this:

We enable people to resonate with the frequency of beauty, love, freedom and power within a universal field of acceptance by connecting with them through photos, video and in person with me, Brenda Lee, Lucy, Red Dog and Eddie. It is through this connection that people are brought to a heightened awareness of themselves and are then able to imagine and create a richer and more fulfilling life.

This field of universal acceptance allows people to feel the power and release of "I am enough".
When you truly accept who they are, you can create what you wish to become.
By thinking outside of the "RUT" and beyond the "ROW" new possibilities are opened within your life.

It is an exciting journey, and everyone here at HKTWH is busy creating theirs while partnering together to enable others to realize the joy and freedoms that are their own. We all want you to live an exciting, fulfilling and joyous life. We are in your corner; rooting for you to start creating the life you know you are capable of living.

So, please enjoy and share in our stories. Brenda Lee, Lucy, Red Dog, Eddie and I welcome you with a smile, soft nuzzle and a wagging tail.

Feel the Connection and Let's GO!!!

"Everything I do with Brenda Lee centers around connection. Is what I'm doing connecting or disconnecting us? Is what I'm thinking connecting or disconnecting me from what I desire, from what I want to create?"

Are you feeling connected right now?

© Tina Thuell

Whispering 8

Great Answers Begin with Great Answers

*"If you want great answers, ask great questions.
Start by acknowledging your hearts desire, say it out loud, describe the details of how you can achieve it then accept it with heartfelt gratitude."*

Do you want "Great Answers" to your current situations, to your major issues and to those things that concern you the most?

How do I............?
How can I.........?
How do I get.....?
What will make me......?

Of course you do! Don't we all?

There is a truth that I experience the reality of over and over again whenever I am playing, working, or hanging out with Brenda Lee:

If I want "Great Answers", I must start with "Great Questions".
And the best way to ask "Great Questions" is to start with "Great Answers".
(This is not some paradoxical circular reference - bear with me for a moment!)

To start with great answers, I start with, "YES".
"YES!" to what is. "YES!" to everything.
I do this by accepting everything as it is - because it is.
This does not have to mean it is as I would want it to be, or that I agree or feel good about how things currently are. Rather, during my acceptance I do not judge reality as *good or bad* or as something that *should or should not* be.
Instead, I say "YES!" to it all.
And within that state of acceptance, I can begin to find my freedom to choose.

I do this because I have found that when I focus on what should or should not be the item I'm focusing on has my full attention and therefore, my power.
When I think that something should not be, I am judging the situation. And in my judgmental state I also judge myself, cutting myself off from the freedoms of forgiveness.
When I say "YES!", I can simply allow it to be. In this tolerant and more passive state of mind, I can then allow what I am and what I want to become.

"To be, or not to be: that is the question." -William Shakespeare

With Brenda Lee, there is no judgment. Everything she sees is information taken in. Not "good" or "bad", not "should" or "should not" be - Just *IS*!

Brenda Lee has to quickly access and accept the things surrounding her just as they are because (as generations before her have proven) her life could depend upon it. This innately instinctive and immediate acceptance helps her to sort and sift freely through the information at hand. And because she wastes no time resisting or debating the information as it comes at her, she can simply move toward whatever feels better to her - moment by moment.

With her it is instinctive.
With us it is an active choice.

So start with "YES!".
A great way to do this is to say "Hmmm, interesting!" to each situation.
Assume a position of non-judgmental observation. Be curious about life.

The next "Great Answer" is "Thank you".
I put myself into a state of gratitude when I say, "thank you" to what I have in my life and to what makes me feel good.
From a state of gratitude I ask for the things I will be grateful for.
How can it be any other way?

But don't just take my word for it - try it right now:
Find something that you enjoy. Find something you are grateful for in your life.
A flower, your job, your health, your shoes, your partner, your country. Look until you find something that makes the simple contemplation of it, feel good to you. Next, increase the volume and choose to feel intense gratitude for it. What do you want *NOW*?

What would you ask for from this state? More of the same?

When I'm in this state of "YES!", followed by the state of gratitude, I'm accepting of myself and I'm connected with myself.
When I'm connected with myself, Brenda Lee can also connect with me.
Once I have this connection - once we have our connection, Brenda Lee and I can create the following "Great Answer": <u>*NEXT!*</u>

<u>YES!,</u> <u>THANK YOU,</u> and <u>NEXT!</u>

"Next" is the natural expression and expansion of the "YES" and the "Thank you" that feels good.

From this mindset, and with these "Great Answers" you can ask the "Great Question":
What do you want <u>*NEXT*</u>?

YES...   I have Brenda Lee and Lucy and Eddie and Red Dog in my life....Yes, Yes, Yes and Yes!

THANK YOU...I'm grateful for the gift of having them in my life. Thank you, Thank you, Thank you and Thank you!

NEXT...Let's have fun! Let's swim in the ocean, run down the beach, play in the snow and explore the forests. Let's show our love for each other. And let's show people how they can recognize and connect with all of the gifts that they already have.

Look around, what do you say <u>YES</u> to?
Look around, what are you <u>THANKFUL</u> for?

Now.....What do you want <u>NEXT</u>?

What would you like to create in your life with Yes and Gratitude in your heart?

Feel the Connection

© Jonathan Jusczyk

Whispering 9

Imagine a Feeling

Imagine the feeling of getting everything you want and more.
And, even though you don't remember asking for more, the "more" feels just perfect.

Yes...this is possible! Not only is it possible to get what you want, it is both probable and perfect! When you imagine the feeling of what you want FIRST and then FOLLOW THE FEELING until the actual manifestation takes place in your life, you can feel your way toward achieving your goals by feeling AS IF they are already in your life

"Imagination is everything. It is the preview of life's coming attractions.
Imagination is more important than knowledge." - Albert Einstein

The key here is to stay with and amplify the "feeling of" what it is that you want.
When I'm with Brenda Lee, I'm aware that she cannot directly engage or connect with the thoughts in my mind. Brenda Lee can only connect with my feelings which are a direct result from my thoughts.

If my feelings are ones that are present and moving toward something I value as powerful, or beautiful, or something I would love to have, she connects with me with an accepting approving presence that is palpable.

This all may seem a little hard to take in at first - so I want you to try two things to see IF this works for you:

1/. Recall an event that happened in your life that felt right and strange at the same time. Something that felt so familiar, it was as if you had already been there before it happened. (You may have heard this referred to as "deja-vu")
Have you experienced this before in your life? How did it make you feel?

2/. Now focus on something small that you want to bring into your life - like freshly squeezed lemonade. Visualize yourself taking a sip. Can you feel your mouth begin to water? Your mind cannot tell the difference between something that is only imagined and something that is real.

Psychologists at the University of Chicago studied three groups of basketball players:
Group One practiced foul shots each day for thirty days.
Group Two was instructed to "imagine" shooting foul shots each day for thirty days.
Group Three was instructed to do nothing.
When tested, group one (practicing shots) improved 24 percent. Group three (doing nothing) had no improvement. Group two, the group that only imagined shooting foul shots, improved 23 percent - yet they had not physically touched a basketball!

Imagine that!

If you want the mouth-watering taste of your successes realized, imagine the feeling of them now. Feel your NEXT now, and you will attract what you want AS IF it were already a part of your life.

There are moments in life when your ability to connect can make all the difference. As I swim with Brenda Lee in the open ocean where it gets too deep to touch bottom, my connection with her is critical. I have come to realize that if I need Brenda Lee to stay with me, I must remain in a playful state while I focus on my feelings and desire to have Brenda Lee engaged and playing with me out in the deep water. I cannot afford a slip-up in focus, letting my mind drift toward any thought of panic, fear, or other worries of what I don't want to happen...because Brenda Lee will pick up on that negative focus just as quickly - and I don't want her to follow those feelings!

When it matters most, I've come to know that my imagined feelings, my IF, of what I want are what she is tuning into. IF I want her to be with me, I must feel AS IF... And that's where the lightness of our connection becomes the strongest.

Imagine the feeling
Focus on the feeling
Feel the feeling
Amplify the feeling

Follow those feelings toward your imagined outcome, and watch the magic take place in your life.

Feel the Connection AS IF you are already there; an imagined feeling...

© Jonathan Jusczyk

Whispering 10

Release the Jaw

Have you ever gritted your teeth?
Do you grind your teeth?
Are you tight-jawed?

Are you ever aware if any tightness is occurring in your jaw or tongue?
Why is this question important?

Many of life's freedoms or restrictions begin in your mouth. By simply relaxing and releasing the tightness we habitually carry in our jaw and tongue, you can begin to create a relaxation response that will ripple through your entire body. And when you are in a relaxed state, you can most easily perceive and move freely toward the goals, dreams and desires that matter most to you.

I keep noticing this simple concept over and over, through many different sources, so I thought I'd share them with you:

Last weekend Brenda Lee had her dentist appointment with Spencer LaFlure of *Advanced Whole Horse Dentistry*. As Spencer filed Brenda Lee's teeth, he explained how the movement and relaxation of the jaw for the horse is crucial, and precedes any balanced and relaxed movement of the whole horse.

While in England this past spring, I had the chance to visit with Derek Clark who apprentices under Philippe Karl. Philippe Karl is a well respected Classical Dressage Master from France. Derek and I were discussing various theories behind horsemanship when he asked me, "What is the purpose of a bit?" Through Derek, I have come to understand that the original purpose of placing a bit in a horse's mouth was to trigger a swallowing/rolling of the tongue relaxation response for the horse. And by beginning the loosening in the mouth and jaw of the horse, you could then transfer relaxation and suppleness to the entire body of the horse, resulting in beautiful movement.

Today in the gym I bumped into a Yoga practitioner extraordinaire who was sharing how he loves to go to the ocean shoreline in Narragansett, Rhode Island, and balance rocks as a form of meditation. I've seen his creations and mentioned to him that they are amazing. He said it all starts with being relaxed and that his Yoga instructor always reminds him to relax his jaw first and then breathe.

I have always instructed people in the gym that in order to reach peak performance you have to first relax your tongue in your mouth and breathe. This will help to access all of your potential.

Think of elite performers who are in the middle of achieving greatness. Their relaxed state always inspires confidence.

Whenever a workshop attendee sits on Brenda Lee in a state of caution and tentativeness, I always ask them to "smile with all four cheeks" so they may relax and feel for the connection that Brenda Lee is offering to them.

Think of the power of a relaxed smile or a soft kiss to communicate a feeling of love.

Our relaxed jaws and tongue can create a relaxation response in us that opens up access to all of our personal power and more.

So smile, say,"Ahhh!", relax and release your potential toward what awaits you!

Feel the Connection

*"Look for experiences outside the box of what you know and inside the good feelings of your imagination and start leaning toward them with all your heart.
All you need to do is say "YES" to the cool stuff life is offering you at the edge of what you know."*

What are you leaning toward right now?

© Jaimie Jusczyk

The Space of Innocence

Where there is freedom to be.
Free of guilt and shame
Free of self judgement
Free of the drama of our life story

Where there is no resistance to be
To be happy
To be curious
To be with your feelings flowing freely

There is love

Brian Reid

© Jonathan Jusczyk

Whispering 11

Put the Cart Before the Horse

Fill your cart with joy, then hitch it to your horse and let it roll through your life and gather the people, places and things that are attracted to your joy.

I'm sure at some point you have heard the expression:"Don't put the cart before the horse."

While this old adage may certainly apply to some of life's predicaments, it certainly doesn't apply to all of them.

Are you the type of person who allows yourself to feel the joy in accomplishing something you've worked hard to achieve? Do you feel the relief of pressure and release toward life's pleasures as you cross another item from your "to do" list?

Or, do you have a list of things that you must do to "make up" for all of the things you've done wrong in your life before you will even consider your own happiness?

If the latter applies to you, I want you to consider another option:

Get happy first!!!

<u>Look</u> for the things in your life that you already love.
<u>Appreciate</u> the beauty that already exists in your life.
<u>Accept</u> that you are already enough and are deserving of all that life has to offer you.

Do these three simple steps as often as possible until you tip the scale toward happiness.

Children do this instinctively.
Can you remember the anticipation you'd feel as a child, knowing that you were going to the beach, a friend's birthday party or heading out on a camping trip? As you prepared for bed the day before, you were already so excited that you'd skip and bounce around the house with happiness. Just thinking about the next day would leave you bubbling over with good feelings. Then, as you began the big day, that state of happiness you were already in directed your attention toward and attracted things that matched your joy.

As a child, you helped to create your reality by putting your good feelings into your "cart" even before you were actually experiencing the event that was creating the happiness.
Fill your cart with joy, then hitch it to your horse and let it roll through your life and gather the people, places and things that are attracted to your joy.

You did not need to fake it! You simply looked for and thought about only those things that felt good to you.

A good friend of mine competes with her mare in the equestrian sport of eventing. As I was enjoying some recent photos of the two of them soaring over jumps and galloping through the cross country courses, I noticed something: She was smiling in every picture. When I said as much, she laughed and replied"Of course I'm smiling! I'm having the time of my life!"
And as I reviewed more photos, I noticed that as much as she was smiling after each jump, she was also smiling before each jump. She was smiling between each jump. She was even smiling throughout her dressage test as she performed flatwork before the judge - hours before beginning the jumping phases that she loved so much.
In other words, she was preparing her "cart" by filling it with the good feelings she knew she would experience as she galloped and jumped her horse later that day. Before each obstacle, she felt the anticipation of sheer joy. During each effort, she felt the thrill of flying together with her beloved horse. And after each obstacle she felt a heartfelt "Thank you" for having had accomplished that goal. And then she would continue on toward the next obstacle, anticipating the joy again.

When I'm with Brenda Lee, I'm made acutely aware that my emotional state of
being determines the quality of our connection because she will only connect with
me to the degree that I'm connected to myself. When I am happy, I'm thinking
good feeling thoughts and she can connect with me because I'm connected with me.

To Brenda Lee, connection is everything - it can be a matter of life or death. So, don't wait to allow yourself the joys you're seeking.

Go out and have the time of your life - now! Prepare your "cart" before your horse. Let your good feelings matter to you so much, that it is as if your life depended on it - Because it does.

Feel the connection to your happiness for no rational or logical reason.

Just feel for it!

© Tina Thuell

Whispering 12

Claiming Your Personal Horsepower!

I asked our **Horses Know the Way Home** *Facebook fans:*
"What are the gifts that horses offer to you?"

I received a wide variety of answers. Our fans feel that horses offer them both spiritual and practical gifts; everything from "Love" to "a Job".

It was the top three answers that really painted a powerful picture - a "Horse-powerful" picture of what we really appreciate from a horse and what we really want for ourselves.

The top three "gifts" were:
1. **Love**
2. **Beauty**
3. **Acceptance**

Combine all three of these and you have all the personal horsepower you need to create anything you desire.

The first being Love.
Unconditional love. The ability to tell you the truth no matter the outcome. The ability to reflect back to you where you are and who you are becoming, moment by moment without judgment on if you are moving toward or away from where you want to be.

The second being Beauty.
Horses are the physical manifestation of that sheer unfiltered feeling of beauty that we all seek within ourselves. In feeling their raw, beautiful essence, we desire to bring more beauty into our lives.

The third being Acceptance.
To be next to a horse is to feel the distance that can lie between knowing you are already enough and any beliefs that block you from this truth. In feeling this space we are drawn back to, "I'm already enough; I simply have to accept that right now." The acceptance that the horse offers us gives us a feeling we can follow to get back "Home" where we know we are okay.

When we combine the feelings of love, beauty and acceptance we begin to touch the source of our true nature. From here we have the power - the "horsepower" - to move mountains or molehills to reclaim our birthright; to find our way "Home".

At all of our **Horses Know the Way Home Workshops** you will experience these feelings of love, beauty and acceptance. Amplify your personal horsepower, so you can harness it and direct it toward creating the life you desire. As any horse will tell you, "You are enough and you possess everything you need to live passionately and live joyously!

Feel the Connection

© Jonathan Jusczyk

Whispering 13

Online and 5 bars strong

Do you sometimes feel disconnected?
Do you ever have a weak personal signal?

Before you run around trying to find that hot spot ...
Before you stand in that spot hoping to not lose that, that, that .....ooops, oh @#$%!
-Get connected!-
How?
-Feel for the connection!-

Your feelings are great receivers giving you excellent feedback about whether an outside stimulus is working for you. Feelings can also be great transmitters, sending out their own signal ahead of time, attracting the situations, experiences and results that feel good to you.

The latter being your responsibility to transmit!
In other words, send out the type and power of signal you need to get what you want!

Your personal WIFI (**What I Feel Inside**) works both as a receiver of outside stimuli and a transmitter of potentialities; your potential yet to be realized.

Last weekend Brenda Lee and I had the opportunity to meet new people by hosting a HKTWH workshop at Rosyln Manor in Granville, Ohio.

One by one, the participants turned their thoughts and attention toward what mattered to them. They began to transmit their "feeling signals" toward their chosen desire, and their WIFI hit five bars.

Not all at once, and not all five bars all the time.
There was the Letting Go of old signals from towers that were now too far away.
There was the picking up on other signals from weak transmitters.

With time and practice everyone was able to experience an important realization: you can set up your own tower and tap into your own signal.

The ability to tap into your own WIFI tower and use it to connect with everything you can desire is the same signal that horses want you to connect with.

Because when you are truly and fully connected with yourself and focused toward your desires, horses can connect with you. And with horses, connection is a life or death situation.

"Most men lead lives of quiet desperation and go to the grave with the song still in them."
Henry David Thoreau

Don't go to your grave never having heard your song because of a weak WIFI.

Right here, right now, start living your life like your life depended on it!
Start living your life 5 bars strong by transmitting your own signal.
Start listening to the song of your life!

Feel the Connection

© Jonathan Jusczyk

Whispering 14

Goal Setting Wi-Fi

Have you ever reached the goals you had set for yourself only to have an empty feeling inside?
"Blah, yawn!"

Have you ever experienced those moments when a goal you had set for yourself came to fruition, but you were still left wanting?
"Is that it?"

At times like these did you question your ability to choose what is right for you?

Maybe it wasn't your "What" that was the problem, maybe it was your "Why"!

The "What" makes an excellent servant but a horrible master. "What" was never meant to be the ultimate goal, only an excellent step towards the ultimate result of every goal.

They are meant to serve your "**Why**"!
They are meant to serve your "**WIFI**", or, "**What I Feel Inside**"!

What feels good to you...inside?
What feels powerful to you...inside?
What feels beautiful to you...inside?

When you answer these questions first about a particular situation you want to change or a goal you want to accomplish, you will be using goal setting as a "**momenting**" tool.

Momenting: The creation of an ever-flowing force of power to create what is beautiful to you in any situation.

When you focus on your **WIFI** (What I Feel Inside!) you will be able to discern whether a particular goal is serving you by moving you toward what you desire or working against you by moving away from what you desire: to feel better!

When you are in line with moving and "**momenting**" toward what feels better, you can use your **WIFI** system to pick the goals that will work for you.

As I stood next to Brenda Lee throughout the week at the HKTWH workshop for the C. Jarvis Insurance Agency and also at the Equine Affaire in Columbus Ohio, I checked my WIFI to see if the goal of bringing Brenda Lee to Ohio for two weeks had been worthwhile.

I watched Brenda Lee observe each individual that approached her, opening hearts and minds to what is beautiful inside each person, one by one.

I watched the light of all brighten as they felt what was beautiful and powerful to them when they looked upon Brenda Lee.

I felt the joy in their hearts as they asked permission to take a photo of Brenda Lee or better still, take a photo of someone they loved standing next to her.

I witnessed the personal "**AH HA!**" moments as each individual in the workshop felt his/her personal power in the freedom of the moment offered by the beautiful acceptance of Brenda Lee.

My **WIFI** was 5 bars strong all week, simply feeling the beauty and power of people connecting with the beauty and power inside themselves.

My goals of what I wanted to accomplish during my trip to Ohio was and is still serving my "**Why**" which is to serve and support my beautiful and powerful **WIFI**: What I feel inside!

How powerful is your **WIFI**?
What is your beautiful "**Why**"?

Answer these questions then set great "***What***" goals to serve them.

Horses, Brenda Lee and all of us at HKTWH want to see you "***Online***" and 5 bars strong.

Feel the Connection

*"Imagine the feeling of knowing you can access all you have to offer in any moment toward any situation.
How would you feel?
What would you do?"*

© Jonathan Jusczyk

Whispering 15

Fall in Love with Your Life

What do you love?
What do you love to do, see, have, hear, and experience?
What do you love to feel?

Is there a space or time in your life where you feel no resistance to being yourself?
A place where you are so comfortable being who you are and who you are becoming that it feels easy just being you?

Maybe it is when you are with your best pals or girlfriends. Maybe it is on the sports field or while walking in nature or hanging with your favorite animals.

Maybe it is sitting behind the wheel of your favorite car, or putting on your favorite blue jeans or a pair of new shoes.

We all have those situations and things that we simply love, just because.
Those people, places, and things that resonate freely within us matter simply because they do. There's no particular reason. They just feel right.

In the last two Whisperings I spoke about getting online "five bars strong" with your physiological WIFI: "What I Feel Inside". I mentioned that what we are feeling matters if we are to continue to move toward what we are becoming. We should move toward what is beautiful and powerful in our lives.

Today I want you to consider the ultimate feeling of Love, and to identify the ingredients that are necessary for you to feel love for something, someplace or sometime.

What thoughts give you a feeling of no resistance?
What thoughts give you complete freedom, peace and passion?

I recently asked a friend of mine this simple question.
After a brief pause she responded: "My girlfriends!"

When she is with her girlfriends she feels free to not only be herself, she also feels the passion and power to be who she wants to become. She loves who she is and who she is moving toward becoming when she is with her girlfriends.

She feels no resistance!

In other areas of her life she is not so clear and not so free. She can feel resistance and restriction from being herself and moving toward what she wants.

In other areas of her life she does not feel her own power to create something beautiful.

By connecting with her feelings of beauty, power and love while she is with her girlfriends she can apply these feelings with intention to ALL other areas of her life where she wants similar feelings.

At Horses Know the Way Home, our first principle for falling in love with your life and moving forward with power toward creating beauty in your life is:

"It's The Release That Teaches"

When we feel better - when we feel the release of restriction and the freedom of movement, we can feel ourselves moving toward what we love and what we are meant to become at that moment.

What feels good to you?
What feels better?
What feels beautiful?

Imagine yourself discovering your personal horsepower! You can create beautiful experiences for all to see, as you "Let Go" of what feels bad and "Let's Go!" toward what feels better!

Giddy-up!

Imagine falling in love with your life!

Go ahead - fall in love with your life like your life depended on it!
That way when you fall; when you let go of all resistance and "Let's Go!" you will fall toward what you love.

What would you do from that point of view?
What would be your "Next"?

Feel the connection to your feelings.
Feel the connection toward what matters to you.
Feel the connection to Love.

© Jonathan Jusczyk

Whispering 16

Awe, Are, Ahhhhh ...

*You'll feel a release when you connect with a feeling and experience of some truth.
All of a sudden "Ah, I Get IT". You won't know if you have a connection until you feel a release. Ahhhhhh...*

Do you sometimes feel stuck or held back, wishing you could not only get one foot in front of the other but actually start walking in the right direction?

The direction of what matters to you.
The direction of consistent good feelings.

Here are three quick steps that will get you going:

1. Be inspired by **Awe** because you are Awesome.
2. Start where you **Are**.
3. Move toward your **Ahhh**.

1. Awe
When you say something, someone or someplace is "awesome" you are referring to your experience of that subject. That powerful experience in reference and reverence to the object of that emotion is inspiring and motivating if you use it as such.

It can also be paralyzing when you stop and judge yourself in relation to what you are observing. When we stop "in awe" of something, we put ourselves behind and below it. Sometimes this can stop us in our tracks. Remember to be inspired and then move toward your inspirations; for it is the movement toward and forward that is life.

2. Are
It is moving and motivating as you move forward in your life; as you move into this moment where you experience the realization of where you are, the truth of who you are, and the awesome power of your potential.

When you realize the true power of who you are in this moment and do not define yourself by your past you will find that right now, you ARE... AWESOME!

3. Ah! and Ahhh.
The power of the realization of how truly awesome you are now can be found in your Ahs!

Ah! As in "Ah-Ha! Now I get it!"

That Ah-Ha! moment when the light of truth goes off in your mind and you understand and own a universal truth as your own. Such as the day you discovered "Asking for help, works" or "Kindness feels good" or "Friendship matters".

Ahhh, as in that sigh of relief and release of energy when you move toward what feels good to you in any given moment.
Ahhh as in "the moving power of Ahhh" when action is taken in the direction of your desires, your dreams.

This Ahhh will let you know when you are moving on your path in the direction of your goals. When another being feels your Ahhh and resonates with you, you will know you have found a partner on your journey and feel the universal truth of "friends matter".

Be inspired by what you are in **AWE** of to become aware of how Awesome you **ARE** right here right now and feel the Ah-Ha! of that, while moving toward the **Ahhhs** that feel good to you.

Feel the Connection

© Jaimie Jusczyk

Whispering 17

Balancing your heart with your mind begins with your Butt

"Life happens. And life can take off and life can scootch out from underneath you just like Brenda Lee can. But even then it would help if you would smile with all 4 cheeks and have the power to put it in perspective because then the desire to create the life you want and finding what matters becomes more important."

It may sound funny, but it's true! Ask a yoga instructor or a dressage rider what their "center" consists of, and it will undoubtedly include a relaxed rear.
Many of us go back and forth and up and down on the seesaw of life trying to balance our hearts with our minds, never realizing that all along we have been sitting on the answer.

When we become uptight in response to a real or perceived threat (or we find ourselves constantly tensed because "uptight" has become our dominant pattern) we are disconnecting from ourselves and our source of personal power.

When life's stresses cause us to become "uptight", we instinctively clench and tense our core muscles. This constricts blood-flow and prevents us from freely utilizing our spinal cord and central nervous system to connect our body. The result is a disconnection from within our physical selves. So, before we can achieve great things both physically and mentally...the BUTT is where we begin.

In order to open our hearts we must first open our hips, otherwise we are like frogs: puffed chests and water tight butts.

When we at *Horses Know the Way Home* say: *"Smile with all four cheeks. Smile with an open heart and breathe."* we really do mean to smile with your butt cheeks!

By choosing to "smile with all four cheeks" you can begin to become relaxed and supple in your seat of power. Then, as you're relaxed and "smiling", let that power move up through your "Gut" and "Core of intuition" to come up and out through your heart.

The flow of energy in this direction enables the mind to focus, direct and release.

The release will enable you to align your present self with the person you are becoming.

When the mind supports the opening of your safety issues seated in your up-tightness or "relaxedness" it allows the intelligence of your gut or intuition to also be heard and add to the power in heart centered thinking.

When each of your faculties is doing its job you will feel at one with your feelings and thoughts in movement toward the desires that the living of your life is inspiring.

You will feel in balance.

In other words, it will feel good, it will feel better, it will feel right and your mind will have done its job supporting your heartfelt intent.
BUTT is where it begins.
Otherwise, you would have a balanced heart and mind on an uptight body. That would not feel right. You would become a successful "Tight Ass"!
Do you know of anyone like this? (Maybe yourself in some area of your life?)

Is that really what you want?

Or do you want to be a success in a relaxed, powerful and present way, where you are open and aware of your balanced heartfelt thoughts centered on the seesaw of a supple open hips.

"If you were uptight about everything that happened to you, you would waste away." - Charles Weldon

Smile with all four cheeks

:-) ....o....:-)

Feel the Connection

"When we accept that our life and the things that fill it are all OURS, then we accept full responsibility for the gratitude, grace, beauty and creative expression and expansion of it in a way that feels better in our hearts."

© Jaimie Jusczyk

Whispering 18

You Are Enough

Brian,
You are enough!
Sincerely,
Brenda Lee

For this Whispering I want to tell you about a little photo series taken during some play time last week. Brenda approached me slowly, as she does when she is "Checking In". She is usually looking for some relief, a rub or an occasional treat.

This time was very different from every other occasion that she has "come in" during play to rise up on her hind legs and stand as tall as she could. Normally, prior to assuming this posture, her energy is very high, very assertive.

She approached me in a relaxed, playful, interactive mode. She had an "ASKING" about her, which I initially interpreted as her desire to be sent out running around the arena.

I would typically do this by lifting the ball off the ground, just enough to get a response, then I would immediately drop the ball.

As she slowly came to me, I could see in her eyes a desire to connect, an "ASKING" that I did not recognize while at the same time it felt very familiar.

She *wanted* to play. She was so full of joy that she wanted to initiate the request to *rise up* to a new level of connection. She chose me and she chose this interaction.

I slowly lifted the ball and she sat back on her hind end and started to lift herself up, as I raised the ball she kept rising with it, when the ball was as high as I could lift, I found myself looking at the white stripe on her belly and her suspension which seemed to float in front of me. She danced there for a few steps then sank slowly back down into our connection. I was full of joy, pride and humility.

She had done this out of sheer desire to play and interact with me.
I was enough, to be her desire and to freely express it.

I was enough for a being who reads the energy of presence, the vibration of authenticity, the rhythms of truth, and the frequency of genuineness.

I was enough for Brenda Lee to want to be with me and that was enough for me.
She had told me that I am enough for me, when I let IT be.

(I.T. Inner Truth)

Do you realize that you are enough?

Will you let "IT" be, so you can see what you are meant to be?

Brenda Lee would love *you* to be Free.

Feel the Connection

© Jaimie Jusczyk

Whispering 19

The Rhythms of Life

Make your own music!!

Have you ever caught your "Second Wind" while doing any physically demanding activity?
Did you know that the term "Second Wind" actually refers to an actual event?
Each of our bodies' eleven systems has its own efficient operating frequency or rhythm (Eleven physiological systems: muscular, digestive, respiratory, skeletal, integumentary, lymph, cardiovascular, endocrine, reproductive, respiratory, nervous…thank you 1st year anatomy and EWU). Each system has its own warm up time to integrate with the others systems. Once this happens then all systems are running together in one supportive rhythm and what a moment before seemed exhausting to do, now feels easier.

At that point running, digging, swimming, playing, or any physical activity you do slips into an efficient rhythm and if you pay attention and stay within that rhythm you will feel your second wind and more. You will now be able to do any task or activity, easier and more enjoyable by staying within its Rhythm

Have you experienced this before or maybe yesterday?

Now consider your behavioral rhythms that are also happening throughout your day.
Working, eating, playing, cleaning, thinking, communicating, creating, sleeping, and many more rhythms that concurrently weave their way through the fabric of your daily activities. The living and breathing of these rhythms create the Biorhythms of your life and you are the conductor of this symphony. You first and most powerful tool as the conductor is your recognition of the best operating frequency of each rhythm.

Just like knowing the most pleasing sound coming from each instrument, each Biorhythm has a pleasing feeling.

It's up to you to follow your feelings of bliss to the rhythm that works for you in each and any activity you partake in. It's up to you to make the necessary adjustments to tune your actions to the right frequency at any given moment to what feels right for you.

At any given moment there is a distinct rhythm to all the individual parts of us. As the conductor you are the one responsible for bringing all the pieces into harmony so that the beautiful song that you radiate to yourself and the world, does so. Start by playing, then listening, then tuning, then amplifying.

Tune into the rhythms of your life and they will sing you the beautiful song of you, and you will have a front row seat at the best musical of your life....

Can you hear the music?
What are you playing?
How does is sound?
How are your Biorhythms?

Feel the Connection

© Jonathan Jusczyk

Whispering 20

To Be or not To Be?

"To be, or not to be, that is the question..." - William Shakespeare

Whether you find yourself in a complex situation like Shakespeare's famous character, Hamlet, or even if you're just muddling through your typical Wednesday, ask yourself this question:

"To be...or not to be..."

As you are a human being, it is your constant state "to be".
And by "being", what state are you currently in?

Is it Anger, Fear, Compassion, Excitement, Focus, Passion, Thoughtfulness, or something else?

What state do you find yourself spending the most time "being" in?

Take a moment to visualize the various states laid out before you like a map. Each state borders another one, and you can travel along from one to the next - but you can only exist in one state at a time.

For the sake of example - let's say you're currently in the state of "Anger". Something occurred earlier today and your mind just keeps stewing over the incident even as you continue along with your daily tasks. Wouldn't you like to exit your current state of "Anger" and move into a more productive state of "Focus" or "Excitement" while you continue on with the remaining tasks of the day? But, you must exit your current state before you may enter into the next state.

So, you must leave the state of "Anger" (which can be as big as Texas) and, needing to move along quickly, you jump onto the Interstate Highway System. As you zip along the interstate, you breathe, relax, release, and cross the state line: you're now into the state of "Aggravation". Not as large as Texas but you are able to keep on the interstate and cross through "Acceptance" faster, and over that state line, you are now into "Acceptance".

Ahh... a much more comfortable state. But, your destination is "Focus" so you need to keep traveling along the interstate a bit further until you've reached your desired destination.

Sometimes you may encounter a detour, or you may need to stop for refueling. But in order to reach your desired state you must continue along, progressing across the map.

So, as Hamlet once posed, "To be, or not to be?" That is today's question.

Where are you, and where do you need to be?
Which route will you take to get yourself there?

Feel the Connection

*"Passion is the fuel that will ignite and maintain the combustion that will send us on our way
toward our desires."*

© Tina Thuell

Look for the Gaps in Life

When you're lost...look for the gaps.

When you're stuck...look for the gaps.

When you feel you can't go on...look for the gaps.

When you are satisfied...look for the gaps.

When you are at peace...look for the gaps.

Everything you want is in the space between.

The Path of Least Resistance toward what feels better, will always lead you home.

Brian Reid

© Jaimie Jusczyk

Whispering 21

3 Steps to a Great A-Game

What is your "A" game?
What is it that you do, that while doing it well, does it for you?

That event, practice, or activity that brings out the best in you and while you're doing it, you feel connected; connected to the best parts of you in an effortless and timeless way.

Here are three simple attitudinal steps that can help you get there more often, in a more pleasurable way.

I use these steps daily to have Brenda Lee, Lucy, Eddie and Red Dog want to be with me.
I use them because going for a walk or a jog with an 1800lb Shire floating on the end of the lead line is just flat cool.
I use them because an 1800lb Shire who does not want to connect with me "sucks".

The same goes for me connecting with myself and it all starts with three simple steps that when practiced, bring out my "A" game every time. And I like my "A" game! It feels good.

All you have to do is look for and apply the attitudes of *Yes... Thank you... Next* to each situation in your life and immediately your 1800lb problems will begin to float for you and become the 1800lb force that supports you.

Yes... Thank you... Next!

1. YES... Accept and Acknowledge and Ah!

Start with saying yes to what is, by Accepting things as they Are.
Why? Because they Are. Reality is, and when we Accept it as it is we start from a firm foundation to move from. I'm not saying your have to Agree with it, only Accept it through non judgmental Awareness as your starting point not your defining point of what is possible.
This is the "now" in life and everything starts from this moment Always.

Yes also Acknowledges Agreement with what you want, with what you have Asked for.
Yes is the Ah! of life.
Do you want this? Yes...Ah!
Does this work for you? Yes...Ah!
Can I? Yes...Ah!
Does this feel good? Ah!

Look for every chance you can to say "**Ah!**" to yourself and to others.
"**Ah!**" initiates your "A" game.

2. Thank You... Appreciate, Award and Awesome

For every "Ah!" feel your Appreciation, feel your gratitude and let it show.
Awards are visual signs of Appreciation and giving yourself and others the Award of your Appreciation will put momentum into your "A" Game.
If you want your "A" Game to Accelerate, let your gratitude resonate through you for others to see and feel.
Let others know how Awesome they are to you in that moment.
And while you're at it, let yourself know how Awesome you are to you.

Even when you don't get what you want, simply say, "No thank you, thanks for asking", and refocus on your next...now.

3. Next... Anticipate and Acquire

Focus your thoughts toward what you want - toward what feels good, by Anticipating the Acquisition of what you want.
Let life Adjust to your focus by following your good feeling toward what you Appreciate now; by Anticipating your next Acquisition... *now*.
Imagine what it would feel like if you got what you wanted... *now*.
And focus your thoughts on the feeling of that state... *now*.
Anticipate Acquiring your desired outcome and Adjust your thoughts toward that feeling... *now*.

AND when you get what you want: "Ah!" Say yes.

Follow these three simple Attitudinal steps in any situation and watch your "A" game play with life!
Watch previously unbelievable Acquisitions or Accomplishments become fun Adventures when subjected to your "A" game. As you Allow All of life's forces to play with you, you will feel the immense power of your true "A" Game.
And that is you being "Authentic You".

Feel the Connection

© Tina Thuell

Whispering 22

It's about what it becomes

Have you ever wanted to go beyond, outside the walls of the life you're living to discover what matters to you?

Outside the walls of your self imposed limits?

Have you ever wanted to find something that you care about so much that it would give you the courage to act upon it?

Wouldn't it be great if that something required you to stay right where you are and make that change?

Plant the seed of your true desires right where you are and let it grow in all its glory for all to see!

"I'm Starting With The Man In The Mirror
I'm Asking Him To Change His Ways
And No Message Could Have Been Any Clearer
If You Wanna Make The World A Better Place
Take A Look At Yourself, And Then Make A Change."
(from: Michael Jackson, "Man In The Mirror")

This was the message from the Once-ler to Ted in the movie "The Lorax".

Upon receiving the last seed of the last tree from the Once-ler and the hope of saving the trees Ted commented "That's it."

The Once-ler replied..."It's not about what it is, It's about what it can become."

IT is our Inner truth, the truth inside our seed of what we are capable of when we care enough to nurture our potential and share it with others.

....but before the Once-ler had given Ted the last seed, Ted had said the magic word that qualified him to receive the hope of it:

Once-ler: "I didn't think anyone still cared."

Ted: "Well that's me: The guy who still cares."

"A horse doesn't care how much you know until he knows how much you care." - Pat Parelli

After receiving that seed and all it could become and "because he cared", Ted followed the Once-ler's directions and went to the center of town and planted the seed to grow so all could see it and all could benefit from it.

We are all very much like Ted, and Brenda Lee would agree!

At *Horses Know The Way Home* we like to say, "Yes, Thank you, Next!" Repeat.

1st: Say **Yes** to what you care about. Everything starts with connecting with what matters to you and saying yes to it out loud. Say, "Yes!" so loudly, that even you can hear it above the noise of distraction. Everything that matters starts with caring.

2nd: Say **Thank You**... When we truly receive something in the state of gratitude, the actual receiving becomes a gift for all to see, especially for the giver. Give yourself the gift of being grateful for who you are and what you are becoming.

3rd: Say **Next**... What we do with our gifts is what we get to enjoy, for it is the growing and use of the gift that shows what it is to become. We can only play with the gifts we have taken out of the package.

And when we grow and expand and express our gifts, step back, take a look and say, "**Yes**!" to what is,

"**Thank you**!" for the gift and "**Next**!" to the becoming.

"It's never too late to be what you might have been." - George Eliot

What do you care about?

What matters enough to you that you will have the courage to act upon it?

What lies dormant in your seed, waiting for you to plant, water and nurture it into existence for all to see ?

Feel the Connection

*"Find the simple moments within your day, your great-itudes.
Notice them. Appreciate them. Amplify and apply them.
Even the smallest great-itudes practiced daily
can change your life."*

© Jaimie Jusczyk

Whispering 23

Small Releases Set Us Free

The answers lay in the softness of your heartfelt desire
Not in the firm grasp of your hand.

We will always have resistance, and that is a good thing. Resistance holds us together.

Without the resistance of gravity we would float away from the planet. Our electrons would spin off of our atoms. Planes cannot fly without the resistance of air. Boats will not float without the resistance of water. And, you could not walk down the street without the resistance from the road against the bottom of your shoes.

We would cease to exist without resistance.

With that said, when we are able to identify and seek out the resistances that work, we find the ability to move freely; simply by working with the resistances of life.

Work toward *What*?

Find something you really want, and set your focus toward the attainment of that goal. As you allow yourself to feel toward the focus, you will also become aware of any distance and resistance that may exist in either space or time between you and your new objective. By maintaining focus and by actively seeking any releases to resistance, you will feel movement toward your new focused objective.

People often approach Brenda Lee with a strong wanting to connect with her beauty and power. With their hands raised and fingers spread in anticipation of wanting to touch her head, they inadvertently reach for her with what Brenda Lee perceives to be a "threatening claw". Before they are able to make contact, Brenda Lee always moves her head to another space where they cannot reach her. Disappointed and unsure of what to do, the person usually internalizes a lack of satisfaction, a lack of connection and then reaches with increased vigor toward Brenda Lee in an attempt to satisfy the desire.
Upon witnessing this moment of resistance, I like to offer a suggestion:

Small Release #1: First, I simply ask them if they want to feel something "really cool". "Would you like to feel a true connection with Brenda Lee?", and I wait for their answer.

Small Release #2: I reach out my open hand (in a neutral position) and ASK:
"May I have your hand?".

Small Release #3: While holding their hand I soften my soft grip even further, allowing the person to actively feel the softening. Then, I ask them to relax.

Small release #4: I ask them to breathe. I take a deep heartfelt breath alongside them.

Small release #5: I ask them, 'Do you want to feel a heartfelt connection with Brenda Lee?", and wait for the answer.

Small release #6: I ask them, "Place your heart inside of your now soft palm. Breathe, and offer your heart to Brenda Lee in a state of receiving."

Big Release, Big Connection: Always at this moment Brenda Lee will start to approach and connect with a whisker's touch. I ask them to feel that and allow the gentleness of it to warm their hearts.

Freedom: Once this intimacy is felt, the resistance in the original approach that disconnected them from what they wanted is exposed. They come to understand how they had inadvertently pushed Brenda Lee away; how their overzealous desire had led them to approach her too fervently, when the sought answer lies in the softness of their heartfelt desire - and not the firm grasp of their hand.

Once they feel the release of resistance they are now free to "just be" with Brenda Lee and their desire to connect - and this feels "really cool". This is fun!

Within the space of connection between Brenda Lee and ourselves, we are set free. It's the small releases that allow us to move with and through resistance, toward our desire to connect with what feels good.

Go ahead, feel for the small releases in your life and start *"Momenting"* today toward your good feelings.

Feel the Connection

© Jaimie Jusczyk

Whispering 24

Blame, Blame, Go Away

> *"Rain, rain go away*
> *Come again another day*
> *Little _____, wants to play."*

Or so goes one version of a popular nursery rhyme. The message is very clear. Dark clouds please leave so the sun can come out and we can go outside to play.

In our lives there are many dark clouds, many of our own making, many from our own perception. In order to shed our darkness and see the light, consider the "HKTWH" version of this poem.

"Blame, blame go away
Come back never, not any day
Little_____, wants to play.
I choose forgiveness and compassion
As my passions are free this way."

I have heard many times how horses are such forgiving animals.
That they accept you as you are.
That they offer us unconditional love.

In my time spent with Brenda Lee I have come to experience a fundamental truth.

She does not forgive because she does not blame. She does not judge herself, others or events as good or bad. She does not have that concept in her being. She experiences each situation for the information provided and acts or reacts accordingly.

When I am in her presence, being accepted as I am in the moment through non-judgemental awareness, I feel innocent.

For most of us feeling innocent is also accompanied by feelings of forgiveness. We think, if we are O.K. just the way we are that something or someone has forgiven us.

It is this feeling of innocence, that you are O.K., that you are enough right here right now. The feeling that you are forgiven that gives a sense of what it feels like to be on top of our mountain, above the rain clouds. From that clear perspective we can see the clouds as just passing through while we feel the sun on our face.

Once we have felt this we can now begin our own journey toward our own mountain top knowing that feeling worthy is our birthright and will guide our way to our peaks in life.

Brenda Lee does not know the words blame, forgiveness, or compassion. She only experiences the energy these words point to.

Since Brenda Lee is all about movement, she naturally moves away from the restrictive and paralyzing energy of blame and judgment while always seeking the path of least resistance toward the free flowing energy of innocence and passion.

"Hey, yay another day
Rain or shine I will play
Because I am deserving in every way
When love and compassion have a say
Big_____, will play today."

Feel the Connection

© Jaimie Jusczyk

Whispering 25

JBT, the Miracle Drug

Just Be there

When our "Red Dog" got hit by a car, he had a broken left tibia, a dislocated right hip and tons of bruising! When we brought him to the Veterinary Hospital, this was their advice:

Pain med 3x a day and anti- inflammatory 2x per day and warm compresses and some joint movement. This along with some gentle massage, lifting him down stairs and making sure he does not lick his wounds.

This were all the instructions I got and oh yea "Don't let him run or slip on slippery floors".

Got it!
Got all of it!

Carpet has been laid on all slippery floor surfaces, I even set up a mattress on the floor to sleep with him but he peed on it five minutes after I made it. I have and will follow all the instructions the Vet gave me and I will add the wonder drug of all healing wonder drugs!!!!

JBT given every moment in HFA doses.

What is JBT and HFA?

For dogs just like humans it is the one drug that kicks in the immune system better than all drugs ever made. It is 100% natural. Costs nothing, (Well almost nothing).
Can be administered in the most minute of doses and still be as effective as massive doses and is impossible to overdose on. Red is in my care and just like anyone or anything I care for this is the only drug I administer. If you know of any person or animal who is hurting, maybe even yourself, just give small doses at first and look in their eyes.

The eyes will tell you when the drug has kicked in.
They will soften as will the corners of their mouths and maybe even a smile may arise.
The immune system is now engaged and full recovery can be expected.

So what is this magic drug and how do you administer it?

JBT is "Just BE There" by the Humane Company Inc.

Given with HFA "Heartfelt Awareness" every chance you get.

Precautions:
1/. You can't fake it or it will backfire and the immune system with shut down.
2/. It must be given from the heart not the head and it must be genuine.
3/. It does not need you to do anything, just want to BE THERE with them and then DO SO!!!

How will you know if it's working?

You will feel it.

Many times there will be no outward sign, the patient will be sleeping soundly and when you are not looking will open one eye and "SEE YOU". That is all that is needed.
You will have a feeling inside that is the feeling you get when love passes through your heart. Many times the opportunity to JBT will, at first, seem very inconvenient.
This is a temporary condition and years later you will feel the results in the most subtle of ways. A sense of peace that you are worthy and that will be the residual benefit of JBT having been left over in your bloodstream for having had the HFA to care for someone when they needed it most. IF you can follow these three simple directions the healing powers of your intention will be miraculous, guaranteed. I have practiced and am practicing this daily and the results are always amazing. So there you go, write your own prescription and start administering this life drug to all you know who need it.

Go forth and heal and remember to

"Feel the Connection"

*"Let your good feelings matter to you so much, that it is as if your life depended on it –
Because it does!"*

© Tina Thuell

Whispering 26

Smile with all four cheeks

Do you ever wish life would just stand still,
if only for a moment ,
so you can get your balance?
Or is it you who need to be still to find your balance?

Balancing your Head with your Heart, Yin with Yang, Masculine with Feminine, Whoa with Go, Past with Future, where you Are with where you Want to be, Can with Cannot, Doubts with Desires, and so on.

Why be concerned with balance?
What can balance do for you?

Balance has power!

Power to move in a way that saves time and adds quality to your life.
Balance offers the power of perspective to see what is happening and to allow you to create what you want in any moment. From a balanced state we can see and feel what is going on in the moment, and only from "The Moment" are we free to create the reality we desire. When we are out of balance, we start to see things from how they shouldn't be (the past) and we react to how we think they should be (the future). Our actions become more reaction, rather than opportunities for creation.

From a balanced state we have perspective to make adjustments from what we do not want, toward what we do want. From a balanced state we can express what we want to create by balancing the past "shoulds" with future "coulds" on the focal point of the present. The present being the only point where true creation can exist. NOW!

How can you get balance to serve you in any situation?

"Smile with all four cheeks"

Notice if you are "Uptight" about certain things in your life. Are you a tight ass or do you grind your teeth on certain issues or maybe all the time? Learn the power for letting go, for gaining control and personal power through balancing your head with your heart.

When your face smiles, your head opens!
When your heart opens, your butt smiles!
Can you feel the connection?
How can you use this today, right now?

When in an unbalanced state we are blinded by our needs to control and react. When in a balanced state we have the "eyes to see" where we are and where we want to go.

Feel the Connection

© Jaimie Jusczyk

Whispering 27

Let Go ... Gone ... Going

Let go of the past crap..."I'm stuck, I'm lost, I'm frozen".
Be here now..."I'm distracted, I'm preoccupied, I'm a dreamer".
Plan for the future..."I'm confused, I'm afraid, I'm paralyzed".

With all this advice of **"letting go of the past"**, **"living in the moment"** and **"living the life of your dreams"**, it is very easy to get distracted and discouraged and disenchanted about feeling happy about the lives we are living.

The Power and Beauty of a Horse

Whenever directors, producers or writers of a movie want to convey a feeling of power and beauty to their audience, they are always well served when using horses to convey this feeling.

I am blessed to know this first hand and share this with you.

The feeling of power and the feeling of beauty can be applied to all three areas of our lives that we are aware of: the past, the present, and the future.

At *Horses Know The Way Home* we always refer to our first Principle: "It is the Release that Teaches".

Release toward "What?" is the ever-present beckoning question.
Before you ask, "What?"
I want you to consider a release toward "Why":

Why let go of the past?
Why be present in this moment, in your heart?
Why move toward your dreams?

...Why?

Because it is powerful and beautiful to do so!

It is powerful and beautiful when you "Let Go" and "Let Gone" of the past judgments of yourself and others.

The eyes that you judge your past with are not the eyes you saw with at that time.

It is powerful and beautiful to "Let's Go" in this moment, in your heart.

As the race in life continues and the runners take their mark...ready...set - GO! They push off the solid starting blocks of the present moment by pushing off from their current reality as they know and accept it.

It is powerful and beautiful when you "Get Going" toward the desires that the living of your life has inspired.

Get going toward your becoming by leaning toward what you want. Lean toward what feels beautiful and powerful to you. This way, even if you fall by leaning too much you will fall in the direction of your desires! And that is a beautiful and powerful "Think"!

The question is: How powerfully and beautifully are your past, present and future serving you with the time that you have left?

Feel the Connection

© Jonathan Jusczyk

Whispering 28

The Bubble

When riding Brenda Lee, she becomes the Ocean and when I surrender into her I find connection.

Does it drive you crazy seeing how friends, family and coworkers get in their own way with the self limiting belief patterns that block them from what YOU see they can become?

Does it make you cringe when someone you love, sees your beautiful becoming, while you cling to small reasoning's that no longer serve you?

Our Egos can get in our way, or they can be the vehicle to our beautiful becoming when we realize our true potential.

Imagine an Ego that goes for it all, toward becoming one with everything and the expression of that.

What would you do with those resources at your disposal?
What if that were true?

What if that were possible?

There is a story, the origin escapes me, of *the bubble* and *the ocean*.
It goes something like this...
We are like the bubbles floating on the surface of the Ocean made by the churning of the sea going waves. In our "bubble-ness" we think we are separate from the Ocean, but the Ocean knows different.
When I look at you from inside my bubble and compare your worth in relation to my bubble, I am seeing you through small eyes.
My bubble is bigger or smaller than yours.
My bubble is more beautiful or uglier than yours.
My group of bubbles that make up the foam of my community is better, or less than yours.
When I look down through the bottom of my bubble and see you through the Ocean of which we are all made then I honor the dignity and integrity of your bubble and the Ocean is pleased because the vibration of that connective energy just passed through it.

Now imagine: What if as a bubble, you let your Ego free to be the shining expression of the Ocean of which you are made, by giving humbling honor to the commonness which joins us through the creative expression of your life filter?

I am eternally grateful for having been able to fully experience this truth on many occasions. While riding Brenda Lee bareback and bridle-less down the beach, in the forest or down a snowy bank, my control is found in my connection to her. She becomes the Ocean and when I surrender into her I find a connection. I feel the connection that binds us.

During these moment, when my life is on the line and falling is an ever present option I find control in release, in surrendering to the Ocean below.
When I surrender to the abyss, a powerful ominous awareness becomes evident. I become aware that the abyss is watching back. Brenda Lee is always there waiting, watching, I am the one who must decide to let go to what is and toward what will become.

This is your decision.
This is your free will to express.

This is an Ego that is short for Everything GO... toward what is beautiful, toward what you love, while the Ocean provides the power to move you.

There are no bubbles in the desert.

Brenda Lee and all horses and animals in their natural state feel this continuous connection to all that is. It is the natural way of things.

We have the ability in our humanness to expand what is by the use of our choices and ability to create.

What if we tapped into the infinite intelligence of the Ocean and start moving toward our beautiful becoming?

What if we moved toward what we love and "fall in love with our life" by falling through

the bottom of our bubble into the Ocean and from there connecting with all other bubbles?

What if...?

Feel the Connection

© Jonathan Jusczyk

Whispering 29

Pick the Pattern that Pleases

Pattern, patterns, patterns... everywhere you look there are patterns in your life.
They make life easier; they simplify tasks so we can have more time for choosing what we want.
We brush our teeth in a certain pattern at a particular time each day.
We drive to work the same way.
We take our coffee the same way.
We fold our clothes, watch TV, exercise, and even make love in predictable patterns.

The question we should be asking is: Are these patterns serving us? Are these patterns pleasing us?

...and if not, then let's change them!

Change them to what?

Ahhh, now you're thinking!

First we need an outcome, a desired result, a goal, a wanting that pleases us to think about. Once we have that in our mind and heart, we can begin to establish patterns that guarantee its success. For example: Let's say you would like to lose 10 lbs of fat.

Simple, right?

Actually simpler than you can imagine!

Patterns for Success for this outcome:
1. Work out at a certain time each day...pattern
2. Drink plenty water at a certain frequency...pattern
3. Connect with a partner or class and work out regularly...pattern
4. Eat smaller more frequent healthy meals...pattern

Work these patterns into your life and you will be guaranteed to lose fat and put on muscle. It has to happen 100% of the time, this is how our physiology is built. We just need patterns that deliver us pleasing results so we can incorporate these patterns into our lives. I know this to be true. I teach personal transformation classes incorporating the principles of HKTWH applied to physical fitness and the results are always pleasing to 100% of the people who apply and surrender to theses patterns in their lives.

What do you want?

What are the pleasing patterns that will take you there?

Answer these questions and get ready for change beyond your imagination, guaranteed!

Feel the Connection

*"When we use our imagination and heart to set the goals
and then engage the mind as our servant to co-create those goals we feel good,
we feel powerful and it feels natural."*

© Tina Thuell

Whispering 30

Balancing the Forces of Nature to Create Momentum in Your Life

Why Balance?

What will it do for you?
Balance doesn't immediately bring visions of power, joy and blissful movement toward your dreams to mind.
It tends to be one of those other words like *moderation* or *responsibility* that has such a weight or pressure to it, that gives it a personality closer to sluggishness rather than forward fuel. A sort of "Do the Right Thing".

Seek balance and eat your vegetables and you will be healthy, and live long.

Balance can do those things and more because balance has power, *magical power*.
When you seek balance in any act, you seek to connect with that which connects us all, and when you get there, time and space seem to disappear. The world and your life begin to make sense in one moment. This is not because I say it is so. **It Is** so and you have felt it yourself and know the truth of this.

Remember being in the "ZONE" in any activity?

A perfect golf swing, tennis shot, swing of the bat, catch of a ball, running under a Frisbee as it hovers above keeping perfect pace with your movement as if it were connected to you. A conversation with a friend that "Just Clicks".
A horseback ride in which you become one with the horse and you lose yourself to the movement.

Just like the Lyrics to the Eminem song "Lose Yourself".

You better lose yourself in the music, the moment
You own it, you better never let it go

Balance has a way of tying you to the "Here And Now" and tapping you into the natural forces of the universe that we all have access to, yet seldom choose.
We think it just happens.
Well I tell you now that Balance is a choice and a state of mind that will release within you the power of connection to that which connects us all and in so doing, bring the power of the rhythms of nature to your experience in life. You will dance with the stars, commune with nature and feel the rhythms and power of the oceans alive in your veins.

Is balance boring or does balance have the power?
The power to bring us to the here and now. The only place we can truly live.
The power to make time stand still.

The power to connect us to the oneness of what we are doing.
The power to create momentum toward what we want because when we are balanced, we have no resistance to our own desires.

Enjoy and share today how you experience the magical powers of Balance in your life.

Feel the Connection

© Tina Thuell

Let's Play Today!

Remember when you were a child and you were bored? Your entire day was about discovering what would be fun to do.

You would invite your friends to join you or you would go get them and together you would make up games to play. You would find ways to have fun, to feel pleasure.
If during those games, the rules or behaviors of others created too much pressure and became more about control rather than connection and joy, you no longer wanted to play.

There would be that moment when one of the children would say, "I don't want to play this game anymore, it's not fun". At that moment even the one who was being controlling realizes: if this person leaves, I can't play or control or connect. So, quick decisions are made to find a way to have fun for all.

We bring this into our adult lives. We have to find a way of getting along with others in difficult situations or else the game stops, the fun stops, the connection stops.
In order to keep the games, the pleasures and the joy active in your life and the relationships of those you are with, seek what brings you pleasure. Then look for the wanting in the eyes of those you are with. If your pressure is driving
them away, make sure your actions are heartfelt and not some old pattern getting in your way. Stay true to your heart, stay true to your joy.

With Brenda Lee, I already have a strong wanting to be connected with her, the challenge, the lesson, the pleasures come from watching my behaviors and discovering what works. When she turns to face me and comes to me with passion my heart overflows with joy and it is this feeling I seek in all areas and moments of my life.

What are you seeking?
What are you wanting?
Do you want pleasure?
Do you want to play?

Start right where you are and be enough for yourself.
Start right where you are and say "Yes I want to play today".

Feel the Connection

© Jonathan Jusczyk

Whispering 31

We Are Feeling Beings

We are feeling beings.
Feeling beings with an intellectual capacity to know and understand our world.

Our categorizations and definitions of our environment have true value to us when they are viewed as servants for our heart's experience; according to the degree that they connect us or disconnect us with life.

The most dynamic and powerful movement within ourselves is usually felt while we are in a state of peace or stillness - often found while surrounded by nature.
For example: While sitting by the edge of a large river that quietly meanders toward the ocean, you can become aware of the awe-inspiring power of the movement that is present in its stillness.

Life's not all peace and tranquillity, but you learn to search for peace and tranquillity even in the face of turbulence.
If you have ever been "*in the zone*" in any life situation, then you know what it is like to be at peak performance and peace of mind at the same time. During a simple event, such as shooting hoops or chasing a Frisbee, you are aware that when you are feeling it, you are at peace.

It can also be felt during a life threatening situation. All of a sudden things slow down and you are the calm at the center of the storm.

In these situations when you "**have It**" you are in a state of peace and stillness while harnessing all of your life energy to move what needs moving - effortlessly. Have you ever heard of a distressed mother lifting a car to rescue her children? It's an amazing and powerful state.

You are One with.
You feel IT.
You are moving IT.
You are witnessing IT.

IT: Your Inner Truth. The truth of what you are and are capable of in that moment is set free to be used and witnessed.

And IT is beautiful when IT happens.

When I'm walking, jogging or swimming with Brenda Lee, I'm in awe of her IT. Her Inner Truth is exposed and I am able to sense her asking for mine. I can give a voice to myself, and I am drawn toward Brenda Lee again and again through this natural interaction.

In the daily exchange between Brenda Lee and Lucy, my heart melts when I can see the honest and truthful connection between them. I am motivated to:

Witness IT
Feel IT
Move and Express IT

Where truth is beauty - and beauty is truth.

Do you see IT?
Where and when do you feel IT?
How do you express IT?
Will you share IT?
Find the expression of your IT and pay IT forward!

Feel the Connection

© Tina Thuell

Whispering 32

Follow your Light

Free to express Yourself.
Free to be Yourself.
Free to choose the life You want to live.

The first two freedoms are freedoms I have offered Eddie, Lucy, Red Dog and Brenda Lee, since the day they came into my life.
I have done everything possible to allow the freedom of expression of each animal's personality and breed characteristics every moment of his or her life.
Not much training here, just a lot of allowing and connecting, resulting in freedom of expression and an intense desire to be with each other and to connect.

Eddie likes to chase Brenda and nip at her tail. They both know this and I leave it up to Brenda Lee to let Eddie know when she is uncomfortable with his play.
As you can see in videos she gives him a warning shot and he respects her space. There is risk here that Eddie could get hurt. However if I could promise Eddie that he would never get hurt and he could live a SAFE life free of risk if he never chased Brenda Lee, he would call that death. He wants to be who he is and express it fully.

Brenda Lee and Lucy on the other hand only want to run, run fast, run free, run together. They always know where each other is and are much more aware of their positioning than my worry could ever see.

So I let them be and time after time I'm humbled by the intelligence of their awareness. Their bond is beyond my understanding and I only get to marvel at the connection they feel for each other without my interference.

For all you wondering why Brenda Lee doesn't run away when she's free to move around on the beach, I'll give you this: if you were loved and wanted and part of a family that looked deep into your essence every time they saw you. Where would you go?

Brenda Lee is free to run on these beaches because we are her herd and no ropes could control her to stay with the force that a heartfelt connection offers any being.

From this place she is free to run, free to fly and feel the joys of expressing who she is.

This is the message she offers us all.

Follow your light to your life.

It is your responsibility and right to live your life your way.

Take all you can from Brenda Lee, Eddie and Lucy and put it in your heart and start today

Discover who you are and let your light shine with all you've got no matter who is nipping at your heels.

Run, fly, chest out, head high, to your light for that is where your life awaits you.

For you have one freedom that they don't have.

You are free to choose.

So DECIDE!!!!

Feel the Connection

"When a free being chooses you, you are at that moment free!

If I stay connected to my heart she follows, if I disconnect she leaves. She has been given this freedom since birth. Many times she leaves and I'm reminded to reconnect with myself first."

© Tina Thuell

Whispering 33

Powerful Vibrations

Have you ever been out of sync?
Have you ever been around someone who is out of sync?
Have you ever had those around you pull you down?
Have you ever pulled someone down with your vibes?

Our vibes! The vibrations we are giving off are very powerful.
They can, and do affect others.
Remember the Beach Boys song "**Good Vibrations**"?
The good news is they also affect us and so we can change them if we want to.

The first obvious step is realizing how the vibes of others as well as our own are resonating within us.
Next, ask: "What results are these vibrations creating in the form of our feelings and our outlook on life?"
Finally decide what music you would like to create with your vibrations.
What rhythms and rhymes move you?

What vibrations make you want to dance?
Find your groove and get in sync.
Find your rhythm and feel the sweet sensations that life has to offer.
Offer the *funky fresh frequency* that feels good to you and offer that to others!!!

Feel the Music ♪

Feel the Connection

© Jaimie Jusczyk

Whispering 34

Get your Freque on!

Life's supposed to be Frequeing Fun!

Wikipedia defines Frequency as: *the number of occurrences of a repeating event per unit time*. It is also referred to as *temporal frequency*. The period is the duration of one cycle in a repeating event. While the world seems to be going crazy, with global economic crisis, global warming, overpopulation, starvation, wars about religion, oil, and any number of events beyond your control, the question is: what *frequeing* thing can you do about it?

Well let's take a look at the frequencies that we have control over and see how we are doing with what we CAN do!

What is your Smiling frequency and duration?
Are you tuned into *wsmile 95.5 fm* or *wfrown 98.1 fm*?
What is the frequency and duration of your Hugs?
What is the frequency and duration of your:

Calling a friend.
Helping someone in need.
Being grateful.
Taking a deep breath.
Saying "I Love you".
Taking a nap.
Patting someone on the back.
Telling someone how much you appreciate them.
Kissing a dog, horse, cat.

Life is about the rhythms and frequencies with which we do those things that feed our souls, nourish our hearts and just plain "Feel Good". So take a moment and think: when is the last time I got my "Freque On", and then get right down to getting to it, you Freque you!

After all, is life not just a reflection of the patterns, rhythms and frequencies that we live by?

Feel the Connection

© Jaimie Jusczyk

Whispering 35

Respect Yourself

"If you are not being treated with love and respect, check your price tag.
Perhaps you have marked yourself down.
It's YOU who tells people what you are worth by what you accept.
Get off the clearance rack & get behind the glass where the valuables are kept!
Learn to value yourself more!
If you don't, no one else will!"

"What is the value YOU place on YOU?"

This was a question I posed recently to all our Horses Know The way Home Facebook fans. At the same time I was interacting with the responses to this post, I was also interacting with the responses to the Bon Jovi song **"It's My Life"**. The refrain in the song that moved me and others was:

"It's my life!
It's now or never!
I ain't gonna live for ever.
I just wanna live while I'm alive
(It's my life)".

Two particular Facebook responses to this post moved me:
1/. "The right to make your own decisions and live your life the way you want to; not by others standards."
2/. "All living beings have the right to live their lives their way!"

All of this led me to two questions
1/. If not you, then who?

Who will set your value, if not you?
Who will you look to determine what respect you deserve, if not you?

2/. If not now, then when?

Pick a time!
Pick a date!

See that by not answering, not picking, you have chosen for others to do so for you!
I have one more question for you to answer regarding your life, your self respect, your value, right here right now!

How good can you stand it?
How good can you stand supportive friendships?
How good can you stand prosperity?
How good can you stand love and affection?
How good can you stand the respect of others?
How good can you stand vibrant health?
How good can you stand "Your Life"?

"I just wanna live while I'm alive."

Your life is waiting for **your** answers every moment of **your** life!
I hope your answers are more than you can stand and you find the legs to handle them!

Feel the Connection

© Tina Thuell

Whispering 36

There is Life after Death

A Story of Love Unfolding

On Sunday night my dear friend Katleen witnessed the passing of Quinn, the Friesian horse that she shared her life with. He was 65 years old in "human years". She was there by his side during the previous three days that he took ill prior to leaving his physical body.

She said her goodbyes and started feeling her loss on Monday and I connected with her on Tuesday. This is the story of that conversation.

Katleen has been interviewing me for the past year to record the story of HKTWH, Brenda Lee, Brian, and why horses, as a personal development model, works so well. During this time we have become close friends, so I wanted to offer my friend some relief from her pain and movement toward a way of seeing the Life in this situation while honoring all her feelings that were arising.

This Whispering is about how I used the story of being human to help her with how to create life in the next chapter of the story of Quinn, her horse friend.

The human I'm referring to is Frank Reid, my father, and how he became more alive in my story of him since his death than when he was alive. My father, like all of us, had many sides to his personality. I often refer to him as a "More Than": more kind, more selfless, more funny and more generous than anyone else I knew. More mean, more violent, more selfish and more fearful than anyone else I ever knew.

After his passing, I got on with my life and decided to pursue a childhood dream of being a Body Builder. During this venture I was often seen in the gym lifting incredible amounts of weight. People around me were amazed and gave me great space when I was working out. Not because I wanted them to but rather because of the intense focused state I would put myself into, in order to lift these weights. I would tap into my father's violence and meanness and move weights that were previously beyond my imagination.

While in this state a funny thing happened. I was filled with gratitude for my father being my father. Something I had lost long ago, wiped out by the states of being on the other side of too much alcohol, and what that does to an already intense personality acting out his pain on others.

Here I was, headphones on, listening to Christina Aguilera's music as loud as it would go and the most obvious forces driving my performance were my father's intensity, anger and violence applied to my childhood dreams in a focused pursuit.
I never asked for this intensity but here it was, available for my use to create rather than destroy. An option only made true by my choosing to direct it toward the life I wanted to create, the story I wanted to write.

I wondered if he ever had this option, if he was ever aware of this choice.

Resentment, loss and anger were transformed through awareness and understanding to gratitude, love, and support and the gift was my father "ALIVE" in my life, lifting me toward the life I wanted to create. My father was alive in my life and I was forty at the time. "Thank you Frank".

Back to Katleen. As I listened to Katleen share her feelings of her loss of Quinn I was moved to see how well she was doing. She was feeling the loss, the pain, the sorrow and she was O.K. with it. She was actually slightly beyond O.K. to a state of satisfaction that she could at once feel pain, loss, sorrow, and confusion all the while feeling warmth, fondness, connection and love toward her companion. She was solid in her authenticity and genuineness. Two states that Quinn taught her were the foundation of *living in the moment* and *following your heart*. As I listened to her, I felt a sense of relief that she was doing well and a sense of gratitude toward having a friend who lives life according to the life lessons her horses have taught her: to be in the moment, to be genuine and authentic.

In her authenticity she shared that she will never get to feel him again. She alluded to her sense of his "goneness", his forever absence from her life, his death. This is where I asked her to think about another option, his Life. I shared with her the story of my father and asked her to consider that every horse she owns or rides from this day forth will be influenced by her relationship with Quinn. She could honor his life and bring him back into her world by feeling for his presence and guidance with every relationship she has going forward and toward the life she is creating. She could create the story of Quinn's *next* rather than his *never*. The choice was hers, she was aware of the option.

I also reminded her of how so many people ask me how old Brenda Lee is, while what they are really asking is how long till she dies. What they don't know is Brenda Lee will always live in my life forever as I hope Quinn does in Katleen's story.

It's not the story of the loss of Quinn; it is the story of the living of Quinn in Katleen's life.

"Quinn and Beyond" the Story of Love Unfolding.

Feel the Connection

© Jonathan Jusczyk

Whispering 37

A Powerful and Pleasing Journey

Passion + Purpose + Partners = A Powerful and Pleasing Journey

Passion; that burning fire within us all.

Each of us has a burning desire that is calling us toward and forward. I know, for some of us, it may only be a puff of smoke, a glowing ember or a flickering flame. Start with some kindling wood to burn (Let go), mix with some oxygen to breathe (good feeling thoughts), add your glowing ember of passion (Let's go), then go grab your marshmallows; our fires tended with some TLC and skill can fuel our journey to great heights.
We can also burn the house down with these same passionate flames.

Passion is in our Heart.
Passion is the fuel that will ignite and maintain the combustion that will send us on our way toward our desires.
Passion that is not harnessed by purpose is a flame that will burn you.
It will scorch your skin and the smoke will choke all who come close to you.
Passion that is harnessed is self fulfilling.

It is the heart's desire and just like love, the more you feel it the more it grows.

Purpose is in our Head.
Purpose is the engine that will harness the flames and produce forward motion.
Purpose is the "What" and "Why" that our passions can serve.
"What are we doing and why do "it" in the first place?", are the engines and vehicles that passion will fuel.

We create great engines and vehicles to carry us through life by being very specific, very particular about the details.

Details count when you are building anything that will harness the true power of passion.
When the two are held in balance we affect the quality of our movement toward.

Not only do we get movement, we are in a balanced state to now direct it toward what feels better to us.

When I'm riding Brenda Lee, I remind myself that she connects with me best when I'm balancing my passion with my purpose or my head with my heart.

I lead with my heart because she does not care what I know until I share that I care. After that I need my head, my purpose to maintain balance and enjoy the ride.

King Solomon said "As a man thinketh in his heart so is he as he continues to think so he remains."

Passion will get you there, purpose will keep you there.

Your heart will connect us and a purpose will keep us connected.

Balance your heart with your head, your passion with your purpose and feel the *"momenting"* of your life move in a fulfilling way.

Feel the Connection,

*"Look around your life for all examples of anything that you feel grateful for
and look for what you love."*

What do you see?

© Jonathan Jusczyk

Whispering 38

To Ponder or to Wonder

Ask Great Questions

If you want great answers, ask great questions.
The question is do you **Ponder the Possibilities** or **Wonder What May Be**?

This is not so much an "either or" question as it is a "which comes first" question.

To Ponder the possibilities is to *think* about your options based on what you already know before making a decision or reaching a conclusion.

To Wonder is to *feel* the possibilities before making a decision.

If we Wonder first about what may be, we allow our heart to lead the way and we explore the unexplored and consider making the imagined a reality.

If we Ponder, we review all that has come before and we choose among already created possibilities. Our head leads the way.

When we Wonder our heart chooses yet-to-be realized realities and we create what might be, then our Pondering can serve our Wondering by providing the actions that we need to take, that *feel* good as we move toward our dreams and desires.

Pondering is the power to make Wonderings come true!
Wondering is the desire, the dreams, the wish that we choose to create.

When we allow ourselves to be full of wonder, Wonder-full, we enter into a state of Wonder and we have Wonderful thoughts and feelings.
Here is where we choose.

Once we have chosen we can Ponder what to do to move toward and forward to our desire.

Thus our head's Ponderings become an excellent servant to our heart's Wonderings and the proper positioning of the head and the heart bring into balance all our creative powers and life becomes Wonderful.

© Jonathan Jusczyk

Whispering 39

Find your Weeeeeeeeeeee!!!

... and express IT

Have you ever felt the pain in your chest,
when someone sees you for more than you see yourself?
Have you ever felt "Not Worthy"
of trust, respect, love, or attention
given freely to you by another being?
Have you ever experienced the unconditional love,
of a cute puppy, beautiful child or,
in this case, a powerful horse and thought
"You're Killing Me"!

At a recent "Horses Know The Way Home" clinic all attendees, as well as myself, went into the dark forest of this reality and came out changed. We shifted to a way of thinking
that freed us all to experience the joy in life by choosing to focus on our *light* instead of our *limitations*. We chose to Find and Feel our Weeeeeee!!!! By focusing on it, then expressing it, we were able to make a dynamic shift.

It all started when I shared my experience
of connecting with Brenda Lee in the forest.
I like to let Brenda Lee run free as often as I can
while walking in the dense forest behind the farm.
She will usually trail a step behind, walk shoulder to shoulder
or sometimes she leads the way a couple of paces out front.

And then there are the times when she will get so far ahead
that I lose sight of her. At these times,
I will stop and listen to the unmistakable sounds
of an 1800 pound Shire bushwhacking her way through the woods.
When this opportunity arises I will position myself
at the end of a long clear path on the trail
and as softly as I can begin to call her name.
The deafening silence in the forest when she comes to a stop,
to listen back, to sense me,
infuses my body with anticipation.

Then it begins, only sounds at first,
of branches breaking under hooves,
as she makes her way back to the trail
as if small trees and downed limbs are meant to be "run through"
for her own self expression, because she can.
I hear her break into a trot, then hit the trail and start to canter,
the thunder of her hoof beat is all I'm aware of,
then I see her and she sees me,
as she transitions into a full gallop,
following her focus to reconnect with me
as if her life depended upon it.
Full charge, full focus, then the sound leaves
and all I'm aware of, is her desire to be with me.
As she approaches I stand in the center of the trail
being the welcoming presence that attracts her.

Fearlessly I hold my ground. I've come to trust her ability
to bring herself to a full stop under her own power.
(in a distance shorter than I used to feel was possible.)

Duh....duh...duh..duh, she comes to a full stop,
head in my chest, a soft and supple presence beckoning
for my recognition of a simple rub on her head
or the back of her powerful neck.

It is at moments like these that I utter the words...
"Brenda you're killing me!"

Now back to the workshop...

During the break,
after I had shared this story with all the workshop attendees,
a woman approached me to share her insights,
with the intentions of helping me be
more aware of the power of my words...
"You're Killing Me!"

She shared her experience
as a Reiki practitioner, (a form of energy therapy)
and how some clients would come in with pain in their legs and say...
"My Leg Is Killing ME".
The energy of these words would amplify
the energy of the injury
and would restrict the energy of healing, is how she put it.

I responded quickly with what I thought
was a very sound intellectual answer
that seemed to show her that I knew what I was talking about.
The problem was:
My answer did not sit well with me.

I told her that what was being killed in that situation
were the parts of me that I wanted to die,
the parts of me that resist and restrict unconditional love
when it gets past my normal defenses.
You know how a puppy or kitten can "get to you",
Get Through to you.

She gently tilted her head 5 degrees to one side
and gave an agreeing Hmmm?,
and went off to enjoy the rest of the break.

In that moment,
the truth of what was happening,
when Brenda Lee sees me and wants to be with me
more than I think I'm worthy of,
became clear.

What was really happening,
when she came thundering up to me
with such power, desire and attention,
was my heart would expand to hold
the increased flow of love and gratitude that I would feel
and the boundaries that contained this flow
would begin to crack and split.
This breaking of the pipe, the limitations,
that contained the flow was what I was referring to
when I said and felt..."You're Killing Me!"

I asked the group:
How could I more accurately express
my satisfaction for the increased flow
of love in my heart
and maybe even add to the expansion?

The answer they gave was...GRATITUDE!
Heartfelt gratitude.

Yes!!!
That was it and we all agreed.

The lunch break was over and we were off
for our reflective, perspective walk in the woods.
The topic of reflection was:
How could we use gratitude to
allow for increased flow of love in our lives?

During our walk,
a beautifully innocent four year old child named Sienna
and her mother chose to ride Brenda.
As we walked I asked Sienna,
How are you feeling up there?

"Weeeeeeee!!!!!"
Was all she said, and that said it all!

Here was this child, loving that she was on a horse,
being witnessed by her mother who was tucked right behind her
and her expression of that experience was
"Weeeeeee!!!!!"

The feeling of love and gratitude resonated
and flowed freely through every cell in her body
illuminating every face that was within earshot.

Her Little Light Shined for all to see,
and we all felt her Weeeeee!!!

After our walk and back in our seats,
we all shared what we are grateful for
and what was our Weeeeee!!!! for that day.

Today, right now!

What are you grateful for?
What is your Weeeeeee!!!!

Feel the Connection

© Jaimie Jusczyk

Whispering 40

Close Your Eyes and See the Light

Let me take you on journey through the woods with Brenda Lee...

Summer has ended and the daylight hours are getting shorter, yet there is a whole new light illuminating my life.

As the days get shorter, so does my time to get to the farm and go for a trail ride with Brenda Lee.

It was on one of these trail rides that started at dusk and ended in complete darkness that my vision of where I am in relationship to where I want to be became crystal clear.
Those lazy, hazy, hot, humid, bug infested days of summer are the time of year I give Brenda Lee a rest. As soon as the fall is here we are ready to hit the trails for the next 10 months of riding and frolicking in the forest. This means I will spend the first three weeks getting Brenda Lee in shape walking and running by her side and then we start the real work. Getting ME in shape, or shaping me.

What I mean is, I need to get my legs and hips stretched and opened so I can connect with Brenda Lee as we ride bareback through the forest. I will give myself three weeks to do this, and will know when I am there because she will move in any direction at any speed and I will "Feel the Connection" as opposed to feeling the tightness in my hips, legs and more importantly my inner self.

We had come to the end of the three weeks and while my hips were opening and legs were stretching, I was now aware of having to "Get Down", become less "Up Tight".
It was during this insightful ride that I rediscovered my happy "Let's Go" then, lo and behold, found my "Let Go". I found and felt that the release that teaches me where I am and how to become one with myself by following my good feeling thoughts.

As we were heading back, a cloud cover had come in and blocked out all moonlight that was illuminating the trail for me. I was "working" on breathing and moving with Brenda Lee in sync. As my vision disappeared, my awareness of the tightness behind my sternum appeared. Ahhhh! There it was, in the darkness I had found my restriction, the source of my inner disconnect.

Was it there because I was worried about the dark and not being able to see my hand in front of my face?
Was it there because I had carried some stressful thoughts from the day and had stored the physical reaction to that stress right there?
Was it there all along and now, because I was no longer distracted by all the visual cues of the beautiful forest, I became aware of it?
Was it there because through my breathing and relaxing I had progressed through letting go of other restrictions and this inner energy was the next one to deal with?

I thought, yes to all of the above and could feel it tighten, compress and get larger just from thinking about it. I could sense for the first time, what it was there all along.
I so wanted to "Let Go" of my inner restriction, my conscious and subconscious blocks that were inhibiting my connection with myself and with Brenda Lee. I want to "Let Go" and become one with her, become one with the ride.

So I started to take deep breaths and through the rhythm of inhale and exhale I became aware of my ability to "push" the energy block down from my sternum through my core into my hips and release them into Brenda Lee. Whewww! Glad that was over, now to keep focused and keep breathing to stay down and stay connected. Brenda Lee's walk was now more vigorous, which required more letting go, more breathing, more focus and more work, I was now sweating and we were only walking.

Was this progress? It didn't feel easier, it actually felt harder. It was this difficult state, this "Not what I wanted" result that had me asking a great and obvious question: What did I want? What did I want?

I wanted to be connected because it would feel good for Brenda Lee and me, and that would make me happy. As I thought these thoughts in the illuminating light of total darkness, I smiled and my heart filled with joy. This joy rushed down my spine and core to my seat and smiled into Brenda Lee with my two big cheeks and I felt her, I felt the connection. WOW, how great is this!

I tried again starting from the bottom up. I felt the size and power of Brenda Lee carrying me in my seat and I smiled with my two big cheeks again and a rush of warm joy came up my spine filled my heart and opened my face cheeks with a light I could see in my mind's eye in the dark forest. Brenda Lee softened and suppled into an equine tempurpedic mattress and I sank into her with a joyous connection.

My joy, my bliss, my good feelings had opened me up to become one with myself and to be able to offer that to her.

In the darkness of the forest I could see what I wanted and what I wanted to become and I became it.

Thank you darkness.

Thank you desire.

Thank you light.

Thank you Brenda Lee for showing me the way home.

Close your eyes, get into the darkness of what you don't want and discover the light of what you do want and feel it now. Let your good feeling guide your way home. Let your bad feelings motivate great questions toward good feelings.

As we left the forest I could feel the density of the air lighten and see the dim lights of the barn. I paused with Brenda Lee right there at the edge of the forest and felt the warmth of gratitude wash over me and wash away all the restrictions of the day.

I thought: I love Horses Know the Way Home and I love Brenda Lee for being the horse that "Does It" for me.

What does it for you?

Feel the Connection

© Jonathan Jusczyk

The Rhythms of our Lives

We're born, we die.
We wake, we sleep.
We work, we rest.
We play, we fight.

Life has many rhythms, we have many patterns.
Some connect us, some disconnect us.
Some move us toward our desire, some move us away.
Some we are aware of, some we've yet to see.
Some feel good, some irritate.
Life has many vibrations, many frequencies.

They can attract joy, they can attract sadness.
They can be music to our ears, they can lull us to sleep.
They can stir the soul, they can incite conflict.
They can create a silence, they can travel around the world.

Life comes and life goes.
What will you do today beneath the rhythm of the rising and setting sun?
Find the rhythms that work for you.

Brian Reid

Whispering 41

Are you Dancing?

Are you Asking?
I'm Asking.
I'm Dancing.

Recently I spoke with Spencer LaFlure, my friend, cowboy, and horse dentist from *Advanced Whole Horse Dentistry*. Spencer and I check in with each other periodically to "feel the good feeling of having friends that feel good having".

Spencer always has some funny cowboy wisdom to share along with a good joke or two or sometimes just a big ear to talk to.

In our last conversation I shared my pleasure of going to my 35th high school reunion and the pain of sore feet and knees from dancing in cowboy boots for 5 hours.

I had shared with him my insecurities of attending this event as I had not been to any of the previous reunions.

In many ways I am not the person I was and wanted to create the experience about how I am now and the expression of that.

So I saw the event ahead of me as a blank canvas and acknowledged my fears and insecurities as wisps of wind that had no weight and gave my full attention to creating a memorable experience that I would be proud of and that would bring pleasure to me and those I came in contact with.

I set my focus on allowing the free expression of two desires:

1/. To be a friend a friend would like to have.
2/. To have fun, free of doubts and insecurities and dance till I dropped or the music ended.

So off I went intent on creating a state of mind that would be in line with my desires.

I shared with Spencer how I was actually able to remember names I thought long forgotten. I felt the good feelings of my youth in the present.
Mostly I shared my bliss in dancing freely with each partner that I shared the dance floor with. I never actually asked anyone to dance and I don't recall anyone asking me to dance specifically. I just remember feeling the bliss of wanting to dance and being open to it all, while letting the music pass through me. The result was 5 hours of memories that will not be soon forgotten.

Spencer, listening to this simply said "sure" in his cowboy drawl and told this story which made sense of it all.

Spencer, who does horse dentistry day in and day out with 1000+lb horses must dance with them daily. The horses stand while he is doing his job and there is a movement of cooperation or one of dislocation. By virtue of the fact that Spencer must do this daily, he has learned the secret to dancing with horses while having his arm in their mouths up to his elbow.

"It is all in the approach" he says.

He was telling this to a group of spectators at a recent Equine Education event and he was demonstrating the wrong approach by assertively projecting himself into the personal space of one of the spectators. She cowered back from him in disconnection and his point was made on how not to approach someone for connection.
Spencer stepped back and spoke of the cowboy manners he was brought up with, and about how the man is to ask the women to dance, and how to politely approach a women to ask her to dance. He also spoke of cowboy ingenuity in "getting it done" and that choosing and having the right state of mind before you asked mattered most in obtaining the desired result, not so much what you said.

While he was about to deliver more of his cowboy wisdom about how to approach someone you want to dance with, a woman from England spoke up about how she experienced this in her life.

Where she came from the asking of a woman to dance went something like this:

A willing man with the desire to dance and the right state of mind would approach a potential dance partner and say...

"Are you dancing?"
To which she would reply: "Are you asking?"
To which he would respond: "I'm asking!"
To which she would offer: "I'm dancing!"
and off they would go.

Imagine that, before asking someone to dance that I might actually ask if dancing is in them.

It was this willingness on my part and on theirs that allowed for a great reunion night of fun.

Yesterday I took Brenda Lee into the indoor arena to simply be, I hung out with her and scratched her itchy spots and watched as she checked out every corner of the arena.

I then asked her if she wanted to play and her state and curiosity opened to me as if to say:
Are you asking?
Yes I'm asking!
Yes I'm dancing!
and we played with a soft connection that was happening before words could describe what was taking place.

I took all of this in: the reunion, Spencer's story and my experience with Brenda Lee and let it stew in mind. I was awed by how easy some things can be at times and how easy it can be to allow easy to be.

Can life be this simple, this easy?

Can I simply have desires and rather than fret about the details simply allow them to be?
Can I simply align with the expression of my desires and in doing so, align with others who are also there?
Can this also happen before the words are needed, making them secondary witnesses to what is really going on: The desire to be and express that!

So I am asking you…

Are you Dancing?

Right now, on the inside, are you dancing your dance?
Can you feel your music?
Is getting on the dance floor simply the next logical step to moving toward the complete outward expression of what is happening inside you?

Then if you wish… Let's go, Let's move to the rhythm of the desires that your life has inspired.

Let's dance!

Feel the Connection

*"When I witnessed people giving themselves permission to use their heartfelt imagination as the source for the story they wanted to tell about their lives, I would see Brenda Lee relax in their presence.
I could see "life" return to their eyes.
They felt free."*

© Jaimie Jusczyk

Whispering 42

The True Expression of Gratitude, Grace and Next!

As I prepare, in the United States, to celebrate the Thanksgiving holiday I catch myself leaning toward the power of gratitude in my life and what is the essence of the expression of this human emotion.

<u>Is it the "Thank You" that I was told to say by my parents every time someone gave me something?</u>

I remember my Mom saying…"What do you say?" to every friendly gesture or gift from family, friend or familiar face and even strangers sometimes. I would say, "Thank youuuu!!!" on cue, like a good little boy, although mumbled in unpracticed attempts at times or with detached feelings from a true connection to gratitude.

<u>Is it the honor and respect I have for the gifts in my life that I don't recall even asking for?</u>

Gratitude for being able to get out of bed each day, being able to breathe, for my health, for the intellect, my nationality, my gender, my opportunities in life, the family I was born into and the family I have chosen as I have grown up. All things that I have but don't necessarily remember asking for.

<u>Is it for the things that have not happened to me? The "It Could Be Worse" form of gratitude.</u>

At least that has not happened to me yet!
I could be them!
It could be worse!

In the spirit of practicality and because I end each day sitting on Brenda Lee for 30 minutes thinking and feeling about how I can truly express my gratitude for her and for the gifts in my life, I wanted to write this Whispering about how Brenda Lee has taught me to express gratitude when I'm blessed enough to remember and feel the pure state of grace that gratitude brings me to and the NEXT that honors this Grace.

Grace, being the unmerited gifts I have in my life. Unmerited not in the sense that I don't deserve them but rather in the sense of I can't do something to deserve them because I already do, simply by being the innocent worthy being that I was born to be.

So there I am, a little child and I have just received **the perfect gift**, something I wanted **just because**.

I said my politically correct "Thank You" to satisfy Mom, Dad and all other adults in my mind.

I felt the grace of deserving it for feeling joy sake. In other words I didn't think: "I do not deserve this and must first go forth and do good deeds to be measured and cashed in before I can receive this." I simply felt deserving because "I Am". For the grace of it!

It is here where the true power of gratitude makes itself available to me.

Here in my next!

This is where Brenda Lee's inability to understand the drama of my life's story, her non-connection with up and downs of the roller coaster ride that my Egomania and Inferiority complex can take me on, comes in handy in getting to the root of Gratitude's true spirit to create joy for all.

Brenda Lee is only interested in one thing.

NEXT!

For a moment, let's say you were the person who gave me that perfect gift.
You were the person whom I said thank you to and you felt acknowledged and recognized.
You were the person who witnessed the pure joy in my eyes of the gift and you felt my joy resonate in your heart as I received it.

How are you feeling right now?
Pretty good I'm guessing but hold on, there's more....
Here is the secret to the true power of gratitude, that Brenda Lee has taught me, to change myself, change my life, heck, to even change my world.

Are you ready?

The secret is NEXT!

Not next as in I'm about to tell you but rather **NEXT** as in what will I do **NEXT** with the gift that you have given me.

If you come back tomorrow and you find your gift thrown in the corner with all the other gifts that I became bored with, how would you feel?

If on the other hand you come by the next day and you find me along with a group of my friends thoroughly enjoying your gift, how would you feel?

Ultimately if you came by on the next day and found me and my friends using your gift to feel joy while creating new and exciting gifts from your gift to share and express our gratitude with others, how would you feel then?

Brenda Lee has taught me it is the expression of my next, the desiring of my desires, the wanting of my wantings, the good feeling expectations of my creations that is the only energy she can connect with. My NEXT and the feelings of my next in this moment.

My next...NOW!

She has shared with me that there is only now and next and if I focus on the good feelings of what I want my next to be and the creation of that, then that is the ultimate expression of gratitude to the giver and the receiver of everything, everyplace, always.

Being a horse, Brenda Lee is always focused on safety first then comfort second. It is the good feelings that she is drawn to for herself and anyone near her.

To Brenda it is all a matter of connection or not.
To Brenda it is all a matter of whether I am moving toward or away from my good feelings.
This good feeling, the feeling of it and the expression of it is the natural way of things.

Babies know it and I need to remember this if I want to feel the powerful creative force of gratitude in my life.

I learn best when I have done something that feels right, feels good.
My mistakes don't teach me so much as they motivate me to find the release that the good feelings offer me and if there is one thing that Brenda Lee has taught me over and over it is... "It is the Release That Teaches".

So as I contemplate this coming Thanksgiving and New Year I will lean toward:

1/. Being properly thankful for all the people, places and things in my life and give them quiet attention and thoughtful recognition. Even to the pains that motivate me to find better feeling situations or responses to exiting circumstances

2/. Bowing my head to the Grace that has brought me here to this earth to express my life as I feel fit for the good feelings and the sharing of those feelings with others.

3/. Preparing for the coming New Year's resolutions and thinking and feeling deeply on how I would like to play with and express the gifts that I have been given and honor them with the deepest true sense of gratitude and Gracefulness that I can have.

The expression and expansion of those gifts for my pleasure and the pleasure of the giver of those gifts to witness.

This year my Thanksgiving - New Year Holiday will be the beginning of my New Year's "NEXTs"!!!

I thank you all for witnessing those gifts that my relationship with Brenda Lee has taught me and the life lessons that she reinforces and sheds new and clearer light on every time I'm with her.

I will focus my thoughts on creating a feel good story that will resonate from me to Brenda Lee and to you, as I live these gifts of life out loud for all to see to the best of my ability.

I wish the same for you!

Tell me please...
What is your Next?
Can you feel the joy of it now?

Feel the Connection

© Jaimie Jusczyk

Whispering 43

Following my Desire to Heaven on Earth

After two hours of bathing Brenda Lee for the Horses Know the Way home workshop last Saturday, it was time to put on the finishing touch: coconut oil.

The directions we received from a Whole Food for Horses website, was to mix a little coconut oil in water then rinse Brenda Lee with this as the final step in making her coat healthy and shiny.

Oh boy, did it work! The next morning at Carolina Equestrian, while getting ready for the workshop, we let Brenda Lee out to graze. Her coat looked like polished granite with velour softness. It had an even sheen amongst her dapples; maybe a little too much sheen. She had a slick look to her. Apparently 1 cup of oil was three times more than needed. No big deal though, all anyone was going to do that day was to sit on her while Brenda Lee was led at a walk.

The following day would be the challenge that would teach the power of balance found while pursuing joy.

The day after the workshop we hooked up the trailer and went to East Beach for a personal development session where Janet, Gloria, Carol, Samra and Katleen were able to ride Brenda Lee on the beach.

For Carol it would be the first time ever on a horse.
For Janet and Gloria it would be a dream come true for the new friends from New Jersey.
For Katleen, who was now a welcome member of the HKTWH family, it was also a dream come true that she traveled from Belgium to create.

For all, the day went as perfectly planned. Perfect weather, perfect friends to witness, perfect rides, perfect dreams come true and with their hind ends perfectly polishing Brenda's coconut oiled coat to a satiny slippery slope that would be my pleasure to sit on as I would follow my bliss and hop on Brenda and gallop down the beach with no saddle and no hands.

As all the "Girls" waited at one point on the beach I walked Brenda approximately 200 yards down the beach to hopefully jump on her 17 hand, 1800lb body from the deep sand beach and let her run free while connecting to her with my heart through my seat and letting the lead rope attached to the rope halter lay loose on her withers.

My first attempt to mount her proved to me just how slippery she was. As I jumped up and on Brenda Lee I had to quickly brace my legs to prevent me from jumping onto and "Over" her. She was so slippery that I almost slid right across her back to the other side, which would have been a sight to behold for the three cameras pointed at me. Luckily I simply slithered back to the ground while looking at the sun's reflection on her satin smooth back which was so slick you could actually see the reflection of the sun on her back.

Now everything changed. My mind, conscious and unconscious, quickly recalculated the current facts and projected to me possible outcomes of this ride I had committed to. My Ego would not let me walk back and my heart yearned for the possible connection that this situation offered.

A tightness formed behind my sternum. I said all kinds of affirmations, smiled with all four cheeks and opened my heart and breathed but still the tightness was there, except now it was more pronounced because my skill set for relaxing into the moment and choosing my state was failing me or so I thought.

I got back in position and prepared myself to jump up just enough to get up onto her and not to faceplant in the sand on the other side. The cold sand at this time of the year does not taste like the spring sand.

Up I went just enough to straddle across her back and lie there as she circled responding to all the mixed signals I was giving her with my flailing legs and gripping hands and arms on her flanks. Round and round and round we went slipping to and fro.

I managed to get my legs over her rump while not sliding off and sit in position on her back.

The tightness behind my sternum was now a solid lump that was also emanating heat.

Breeeeeeathe!!! Breeeeeathe! I was using all my skills to relax, and calm down when I had a quick thought that was followed by an instant release. If I could ride this how cool would that be. How connected would I have to be to be one with her in this situation?

Everything I do with Brenda centers around connection. Is what I'm doing connecting or disconnecting us? Is what I'm thinking connecting or disconnecting me from what I desire, from what I want to create?

That momentary thought of joy that had slipped into the moment had brought me enough release, enough pleasure that I had something to focus on. I followed that good feeling and turned my focus and with it Brenda's focus back toward the "Girls" and off we went. Within three strides we were off and galloping and I was only aware of my bliss, the beach itself was flying below me as if Brenda were stationary and the world was traveling past us. I let the rope lay on her back and lifted my arms to the side while feeling the cool wind against my sun warmed face.

Then everything went silent and all I was aware of was floating across the beach. No Brenda Lee, no Brian, just movement.

We came to a smooth transitioning stop near the photographers who were full of beautifully helpful suggestions for the next time I did that: *"Your head wasn't up, you were looking at the ground, your chest was not out in front, sit taller next time."*
All from my support team who know the quality with which I want to ride and all feeling the freedom to express. All suggestions that I loved because they were leverage for me to do that again. I did not know why at the time but I so wanted to get right back down the beach and try that again.

As I walked back to where I started and beyond I became aware of the something strange and transformational.

All during the ride, as a matter of fact, within the first two strides the warm tight lump in my chest that all forms of relaxation, affirmations and meditations could not remove had disappeared. My focus on the joy, bliss, and good feeling I might experience removed that which I could not remove my self.

By feeling the beauty of the ride I was about to experience before I actually rode, I aligned myself with the perfect ride that awaited me.

I got back on Brenda Lee's back again with the same tightness patterned response weighing in my chest, except this time I gave it no mind. Instead I gave my mind to the desires before me that my life to this point had inspired and off we went. I simply turned and smiled at the distance before me and allowed myself to be transported to the blissful ride, as Brenda Lee and I ran down the beach catching up with the beautiful moments that my desires had waiting for me.

This time I was so present that I had the clear focus to remember to lift my head, smile, surrender into Brenda Lee and be conscious of what it feels like to be one with that which connects us all.

I do not know what heaven is like but I do know what heaven on earth feels like.

But more importantly Brenda Lee and her coconut oiled back had given me the recipe, the key and the formula for recreating this experience, for finding my way home.

And that formula is:
LET'S GO and follow the desires that the living of my life inspires!

With the us in "Let's" being me, Brenda Lee, and the "Girls " witnessing and the great witness of all that is setting this up.

Feel the Connection

© Jaimie Jusczyk

Whispering 44

Follow your Heart

Balanced...on the Path of Least Resistance!

In this photo, Brenda Lee was led to the far end a long fairway on an abandoned golf course, by someone other than me. Photographer Jaimie Jusczyk positioned herself in the middle of the fairway and off to one side to capture Brenda Lee running toward me. I positioned myself at the far end of the fairway in plain sight so Brenda Lee could see me and thus create "The Draw"...The forces of a heart felt desire to connect.

Brenda Lee's desire to shorten the distance of her connection between us was strong.
Her heart has always been free to feel what she wants without resistance. Imagine that for a moment. One ton of freedom to follow one's heart's desire, released toward its focus.

Can you see the heartfelt focus?

Forward and toward, energies all in balance along with the immovable earth that Brenda Lee is pushing off against to create floating freedom of forward momentum in balance.
Not balance that creates a static non moving state but rather the balance of grounding and explosive forces that create a circular motion that propels electrons around a nucleus of an atom and planets around the sun. In this case: hooves below a silent centered torso.
By focusing on her desired outcome Brenda Lee's mind finds the "Path of Least Resistance" toward her desired outcome so she can fly!!!

Imagine what it is like to be on the receiving end of this force?
Imagine what it is like to have the raw power of nature focus on you as the reason for moving?

What is your heart's desire?
Are you willing to find the "Path of Least Resistance" toward it?
Are you willing to have the raw, wild force of nature as your partner in achieving your desires?

Feel the Connection

Whispering 45

Winning the Race of Life, Right Now!

Ready, Set, Go!

Simple as 1-2-3... really!

What if winning at life could be as simple as 1-2-3, Ready... Set... GO!

Well, it can be and I've found that it is easier than I thought.

Every time my life is going the way I want it to, I find myself following three simple actions, three simple ways of being and I'm always satisfied with the results these principles produce.

No more fighting to get other people and events in my life in line to satisfy me.
No more going against the grain, only to feel as if I've accomplished something of value.
No more nose against the grindstone, just to feel discomfort so I feel satisfied.

A new way of being that was always present every time life aligns for me, naturally.

So do you want to race? Great! Let's go...

1. GET READY... Let your heart be the master.

If we are going to race we will want to know where the finish line is, and why we are racing.
Let your heart set these goals for you.
Let your heart answer the "*Why of Life*".
Allow your heartfelt desires, wants and wishes and the expression and expansion of them be your reason for getting on the line, for showing up.
Let the force of your heart be the energy that propels you toward your goal.
Don't worry about your head, the heart is an excellent master and will always include the head in all decisions.

2. GET SET... Find your balance.

You have heard it many times before, all things in balance.
So there is a state to launch from, to push off from, in any direction, because all energies are ready for you and available for you.
You have heard of this before in many forms, Yin/Yan, Black/White, Positive/Negative.
It is the balancing of these forces in a circular motion that allows their force to be available, to move you in the direction of your focus, and hopefully that focus is through the eyes of your heart.

3. Go... Go and follow the path of least resistance.

When you are following your heart in a balanced way then the path of least resistance will be the one that will be true.
Look for the "Yes" and move away from the "No".
Feel for the "Yes" in life and when you feel its joy, give gratitude for its reception which will bring you right back to your NEXT, your heart's desire.

Simple as 1-2-3, Ready... Set... Go, or

Yes, Thank you , Next.

Yes... to receiving what you wanted!
Thank You... to the force that delivered it!
Next... toward your new desire from a new perspective!

You Win!!!

Feel the Connection

*"When you focus on the feelings of what is behind you, you will get more of
what is behind you!*

If you don't like that feeling, turn around."

© Jaimie Jusczyk

Whispering 46

How do you experience others?

How do you see life from your perspective?

Others in this photo...Brenda Lee the Shire horse and Lucy the Yorkie.

While Brenda Lee always knows where Lucy is at all times, the perspective of Lucy is quite different.

As a child I knew my father by the size of his hands and his work boots.
I knew my mother by her hugs with my face buried in her belly.

Lucy and Eddie know Brenda Lee by her four big white feathered feet that always seem to know where they are.
They never really make eye contact with her.
It is the four thundering hooves that delicately respect their space while feeling for them as they run through the woods or down the beach.
These hooves seem to reach out to them the way my father's hand would reach out to me when I was three or four at any crowded venue.
Just find the hand and I'm safe.
Just follow the sentient hooves and we are part of the action.

Can you feel their connection?

How do you experience the ones who are in your life?
What part of them do you connect to?

Feel the Connection

© Jaimie Jusczyk

Whispering 47

Fulfilling Freedom of Witnessing a Flying Shire

*Feel the connection to your freedom to imagine
and fuel the fire to make your dreams come true!*

Approximately seven years ago Brenda Lee stepped on a nail that went through her left front hoof and stuck in her coffin bone, (the bone in a horses hoof) and infected the coffin bone. (There is a reason they call it the "coffin" bone.)

Undetected and misdiagnosed for 6 weeks, the infection grew and Brenda Lee ended up in Tufts University late one night to receive X-rays and a venogram to determine the extent of her ailment. A piece of the infected coffin bone about the size of the tip of your pinkie finger had broken off and was floating in infected tissue below the coffin bone which had delaminated from the hoof and now was rotated.

I stood in front of all the high tech computer screens seeing the digital results of the damage and the complete lack of any veins or arteries on one side of her hoof. Six concerned faces were focusing on me while also looking toward the floor.

Small percent chance of living and even smaller percent chance of being sound, was the diagnosis!

What do you want us to do? This was the question they were asking me.

In order for her to be healthy again she would have to overcome:
1/. A systemic infection.
2/. A bone infection.
3/. Founder and rotation of the hoof.
4/. Have her flexor tendon cut and grow back.
5/. Survive recovery from surgery.
6/. Not founder on the good hoof.
7/. Grow new hoof.
8/. Loose 400lbs. She was 2100lbs at the time.
9/. Endure a long two to three year recovery.

Well, she/we did all that but still there were foot issues.

Shoes with wedges, glue on shoes, shoes, no shoes, boa boots, thrush, balancing her hoof, thin soles, barefoot trims for two years and still she was *ouchie*. She always found a way to walk on the soft banks of the trails or she could find relief with the occasional beach runs in deep sand.

Long gone was the hope of ever seeing her totally free spirit galloping unrestricted which I had come to know during our first seven years together. The thundering gallop that would end with floating prances of weightlessness. Gone was the happy expression of a pain free body, or so I thought...

Last Sunday I took Brenda Lee, her paddock mate Sasha, my niece Cilla and little Lucy to an abandoned golf course for a photo shoot with Jonathan and Jaimie.

For the previous 5 weeks, Brenda Lee had been wearing new horseshoes for the first time in two years because of her thin soles. (For all you barefoot people, of whom I'm one, I could no longer stand to see her in pain and opted to give her relief instead).

The new farrier, Jeff Trask, had installed leather pads between her soles and the shoes on the front feet. (Brenda Lee is still barefoot on the hind feet) The pads were there to cushion the soles from the stones and rocks she travels on. It had been 5 weeks and we were riding each night for about an hour down the center of the trails, mostly walking, with some trotting. The only cantering she was doing was in the sand arena. I was extremely happy at this point. My happiness would go to new heights very soon.

We walked to the golf course and set up. Jonathan and Jaimie positioned themselves at their preferred vantage points along a long hill. Cilla and Sasha walked to the top of the hill just at the top, just in sight for Brenda Lee to see them. Lucy and I stayed at the bottom with Brenda Lee until everyone was ready. I asked for a big thumbs up from everyone and then turned to Brenda Lee.

If she still felt sore, she would walk with me as I caught up with everyone.

If she felt O.K., she would trot up the hill to Cilla and Sasha, Lucy at her heels, and stop in the lush green grass to graze.

If she felt recovered, she would canter up the hill.

If she felt healthy she would gallop up the hill.

As I reach up to undo her halter to set her free, I had mixed emotions about what I might witness. And then, there it was, soft at first, so soft I almost didn't want to hear it, then loud enough just for my ears.

Brenda Lee was whimpering. Not out of pain, but out of joyous anticipation. Her wildness wanted out.

I reached up to undo her halter still not allowing myself to feel what might be and she gave me another sign.

She started pounding her front left hoof to the ground. She was ready and I was happily remembering what this meant.

The fire was back in her spirit and her body. She was ready to set it free. I knew Jonathan and Jaimie would see and feel what I knew was inside waiting to get out for the past 6 years.

It is the *release that teaches* and this release was about to teach me that if you always keep believing there is always hope.

I released the halter and as her head slipped free, I heard one last whimper and caught a glimpse of her eye as she turned toward the open space. *"Thank you"* was all I felt.

Off she went, galloping at first, then thundering, then flying, and when her tail lifted so did my heart. Brenda Lee was back in mind, spirit and body and she was flying free.

She flew up the hill to Cilla, turned and ended her flight in a floating trot of weightlessness. She lifted and arched her neck and puffed out her chest and let loose a snort for the whole forest to hear.

"I am" was all she said and the forest and all its inhabitants knew it.

Brenda Lee then turned her head back to the bottom of the hill where I was standing. My heart was full and flying free, for I had been with her every step of the way up that hill and to this point of freedom. I could feel her fire burning in my belly. Brenda Lee was back and this time I had witnesses to share it with.

We spent the next two hours letting her run free. Her wildness came back and she would lead the way patrolling the perimeter ahead like any powerful alpha mare. We were her herd until the end when she would give the leadership back to me in a grateful moment of appreciation between us both.

I'm glad I got to share this with my niece Cilla and I am especially glad that Jonathan and Jaimie photographed the day so we could share it with you.

I hope you feel the connection to your freedom to imagine and fuel the fire to make your dreams come true.

Feel the Connection

P.S.

The entire time Lucy ran back and forth between Brenda and me. Up and down the hills in grass that was twice her size covering four times the ground that we all traveled. She was smiling with all four cheeks and an open heart the entire time. Her freedom and fire were just as fulfilling to witness as Brenda Lee's.

P.P.S.
To be in the presence of free beings fully expressing themselves without restriction wakens something in the depth of our being that is more valuable than gold and more precious than diamonds and free for us all if we just look for it. But you must look with the eyes of your heart.

Can you see?

© Jaimie Jusczyk

Whispering 48

Patterns that Serve

Kick Start your Pleasing Patterns

On a beautiful day in Spring our HKTWH Photographer Jaimie and I headed to the farm to load Brenda Lee in the trailer to go the beach to film "A Kick Start to Freedom".

This would be the final chapter for one year of the HKTWH Academy curriculum.

We both noticed how calm and like glass the bay was as we drove over the Jamestown Bridge.

Since the topic of our shooting was to be about **patterns**, Jaimie and I talked about the **pattern of peace** and tranquility that the glassy bay surface offered us. Later when we got to the beach, the pattern of the waves was mild and beautiful to watch with the varying colors and shapes that were easy on the eyes. I thought *"what a **beautiful pattern** to watch; great eye candy, so pleasing and pleasurable to the eyes"*.

We quickly set up the cameras and got right into filming and decided to focus less on content and more on play time and just being with the horses and dogs enjoying the beautiful day. So we let Brenda Lee and the dogs run free for some seriously fun playtime with no agenda. As Brenda Lee ran free, seemingly weightless, galloping down the beach, I became lost in the sensation of freedom and the joy of watching it. When they came to a stop I looked at the waves and imagined a larger **surf pattern** where I could feel the same sensation of being carried weightlessly over a distance of joy, body surfing in another **playful pattern** offered up to me from the Ocean. The wind had continued to increase and Brenda Lee was feeling her Oats, so to speak. She was quite full of herself and really wanted to cut loose. So up on top I got and she took off like a shot, first chasing Eddie Spaghetti , then blowing right by him, what exhilaration, what power!

When we came to a stop just past Jaimie and the cameras, I imagined a different pattern of the sea: one in which the awesome power of the Ocean shows itself after a big storm. No playing in that, just sit in awe and observe another of Mother Nature's **powerful patterns.**

Patterns of Peace
Pattern of Play
Patterns of Power

They all brought joy to me just thinking about them and experiencing them. It was at this moment that my mind shifted to the destructive patterns of the Ocean. The Tsunami that had just hit Japan and had traveled across the Pacific Ocean at 500 mph. One ripple or maybe a couple, traveling many thousands of mile only to stop when it hit a continent.

WOW! Is there anything more powerful than patterns for bringing such variety of experiences into our lives?

All our patterns started out with the same intention, to bring pleasure or relief to our lives. Even the Tsunami was caused when the tension in the earths crust was released.
You can't blame the crust of the earth for building up pressure as it moves through the shifting effects of life on earth over time any more than you can blame yourself or anyone for the pressures that build up and release themselves in our lives. All you can do, if you want to keep moving toward your desires, it to **kick aside** the patterns that no longer serve you or bring you pleasure and **kick start** the ones that do. Do this and your life will be like riding a wave or flying down the beach on a beautiful powerful horse. Don't do this and the patterns of life will wash over you like a Tsunami and take back into the sea all you have created, in one fell swoop.

Patterns have great power.

Recognize and keep the ones that work, **kick start** new ones that you want and **kick** the ones that don't, right in the ass and out of your life!

That is what a **"Kick Start to Freedom"** is all about!

So what do you say, are you ready to **"Kick It"** ?

Feel the Connection

"Free to express Yourself.

Free to be Yourself.

Free to choose the life You want to live."

What are you going to do today that will express who you are?

© Jonathan Jusczyk

Whispering 49

The Art of Let's Go

It's the Release that Teaches.

Let's look at the **Act of Let Go** or the **Art of Let's Go**.

1/. **The Act of Let Go.**

You wish to let go of some bad habit, a bad relationship or a way of living that does not bring you pleasure, peace of mind or personal satisfaction. You identify all the reasons this situation is in your life, you analyse all the factors and you find yourself investing all your time, energy and focus on what you wish to let go of.

Can you see and feel, how your investment of time energy and focus in your let go becomes the glue that binds you to that which you wish to let go of?

Do you really think that you can give anything enough attention so that it will magically go away?

2/. **The Art of Let's Go.**

In the Art of Let's Go you simply feel for and focus on your relief. What feels better, what feels natural to you in any moment in time? One way of thinking of "Let's Go" is letting go toward what you want, releasing yourself toward what feels better, what moves you toward a better feeling or a predetermined goal. Another way is perceiving the words "Let's Go" or "Let Us Go". When someone you care about says to you:

"Let's Go", they are implying that there is a predetermined destination that you both wish to go toward. This predetermined place is calling you forward and toward it with feelings of relief and release. This is why at **Horses Know The Way Home** our first principle, that all the rest are built upon is:

"*The Release that Teaches*".

If you follow your good feelings of release, you will not only achieve your desired outcomes, you will enjoy the journey. As a bonus you will be given a pleasurable reason to let go of what has been holding you back so you can move toward your desires rather than letting go for *letting go's* sake.

Consider this...

Do your really learn from your mistakes or do you learn when you have done something right?

When we do something right we feel better. It is this *"release that teaches"* us that we have gotten it right. The release is the "Ahhh!" in "Ahhh! Now I get it!"

Our pain motivates us to find our path in life.

Our release teaches us when we are on our path.

Feel for and find your relief!

Find and feel for your release!

Feel the Connection

© Jaimie Jusczyk

Whispering 50

You are listening to HKTWH FM radio!

Any and all frequencies that feel good to you, right here, right now radio!

Just tune into your favorite feelings of this moment and sit back
and enjoy the music that moves you.
Whether you are feeling sad or glad,
Up or down,
Ready to move or sit back and relax,

We have the rhythm that will sync with your feelings in the moment and sooth you
while moving you to the beat of your heart.
All your feelings will be amplified for you to feel.
All your vibrations will be amplified, so you can distinguish what feels better.

So *find* your feelings,

Feel your feelings,

Connect to your feelings.

Feel the connection to that which connects us all.

And groove,

Let loose,

Let the music move you,

Release to the rhythm of your soul and sing your song for all to hear!
Especially yourself!

Hear and enjoy your song.

We have the songs for your now and your next!
All right here at HKTWH radio.
Just turn the dial 'til you feel better and that will be us.

Ready to move you.
Ready to groove you.

To the beat, the rhythm, the song in your heart that feels good now, for you to sing.

This is your station, your vibration,
Let the rhythm move you, and groove you.
Brenda Lee wants to hear only one song from you,

Only one frequency that fits.
She wants to hear your authentic song.
She wants to feel your genuine vibration.

For it is only here and now, on your channel that she can connect with you!

And to her, connection is LIFE!

So release yourself to the rhythms that move you.
Right here, right now
On HKTWH radio.
That is Horses Know The Way Home Radio.

Any frequency on your dial that "Does IT" for you.

What do you want to hear?
What do you want to play?

Feel the Connection

© Tina Thuell

Whispering 51

Smile While you Walk

:)--o---:)

"Smile With all four Cheeks"

A walk in the woods with friends inspires thoughts of relaxation, peace, and connection to Mother Nature. But what if you are not connected to yourself first?

What if you are not "At Home" with yourself?

What if, as you go on your walk you are up-tight, upset, wound a little tight, or to be crude, you are a tight ass. These words are accurate descriptions of our state and where we are holding or blocking our energy in our body.

If we want to enjoy our walk as well as our friends, it would help if we could "Let Go", relax, chill out, or release all our tension so we can be present with ourselves, others and Mother Nature.

The following is a description of how I chose to release my tension and connect with myself and my friends, Brenda Lee and Lucy as I walked through the woods.

While walking in the woods with Brenda Lee I could see her looking back at me with one soft eye then the other. She always had me in her gaze, every time I looked up at her. On one occasion I smiled to her with my facial cheeks, just to let her know how happy I was that she was watching.

While smiling through my face I could tell the difference between the relaxation in my face and the tension in my abdomen and lower body. I decided to let my smile float down through my body till I felt a release in my "butt" cheeks. Wow! I did not realize how uptight I had been until I felt this release. It felt good, I felt calm and most surprisingly, I felt at ease. I repeated this smiling upstairs then downstairs exercise while acknowledging Brenda Lee and letting her feel my new sense of connectedness to my whole body.

She was already there, so much so that I knew she knew I was connected before I did. I felt so confident in this new found connection that I decided to use it as my invisible lead line while walking with her. I would count on my connection to my own inner joy radiating out, to be what would connect us as we walked (Instead of a halter or lead line).

Was I crazy?

On a couple of occasions while Brenda Lee was out in front, she would try to circle back around me and head back the barn and the thick green grass pasture that awaited her there. Whenever she did this I smiled with my butt cheeks first, by releasing and relaxing then letting this joyous release rise up through my body to my face cheeks and "Smile with All Four Cheeks". I would then attach this peaceful, joyous state to my "wanting" her to come to me and like some powerful electromagnet it worked.

She would turn sharply and come running to me rather than the green pastures of home.

Once I was at home with myself, I was enough for Brenda Lee.

Horses really do know The Way Home.

Feel the Connection

© Tina Thuell

Whispering 52

Let What Matters Become Matter!

You matter! And what matters to you, matters.
You are already enough.
Nurture what matters to you until it becomes matter.

There is no more for you to do in order to become a deserving person.
Let grace live freely in your life.
Live a graceful life.

This message of "grace" is shared with me through Brenda Lee every time I'm in her presence. This grace is an unmerited gift from her. It is unmeritable because I do not have to do anything in order to deserve it - *I already deserve it*.

I already deserve it because Brenda Lee accepts me "as-is".
As Brenda Lee and I play together, it is often within this state of unconditional acceptance. It is with her gift of grace that I am able to experience this important self acceptance realization: **"I matter"**

There is a song lyric that comes to mind: "*Learning to love yourself is the greatest gift of all*'. (Whitney Houston)

The key word there is **Learning**.
Learning to love the self that is connected to everything, while accepting the self that wants to be separate. Or, **Learning** to love the self that surrenders to and connects to everything, while also being aware of the self that controls and disconnects. This surrendering, connecting and graceful self is the one that Brenda Lee connects with. When we are in this accepting state, we know that we matter. And what matters to us actually becomes matter. This is the state where *dreams come true*.

So if you want to know, "What's the matter?"
The answer is: **YOU**!

Not only do you matter, but what matters to you, matters! And very soon, if you allow and look for it you will see what matters to you, become matter.

You will have made your dreams become matter because you realized - as Brenda Lee already realized - that you are already enough.

You matter.

Feel the Connection

© Jaimie Jusczyk

Just Breathe

Something so simple, so easy, so free and so powerful,
and yes we need reminding that breathing can open us to beauty and joy like no other action.

Allowing the one element of life that we cannot live without for more than three
minutes, to openly pass through you, not only sustains life,
it also opens our hearts to what is next, allowing the energies of our "dreams come
true" to flow freely through us into reality.

And, YES we still need reminders for this simple act that we all take for granted yet
has the power to transform our lives!

Just breathe and Feel the Connection

Brian Reid

© Jonathan Jusczyk

BonusWhispering 1

Beating the "Blah's"

I awoke today not feeling great - not feeling terribly bad either, just sort of malaise, sort of "blah". I had a lot planned for today and was hoping for the energy or the motivation to "get it done".

I tried focusing on the things I was grateful for, the things I loved, but no change in my feelings occurred - or so I thought.
I headed out into the day determined to be productive and at the same time take care of my well-being.

I parked my van at the edge of a grassy field. It was cluttered and chaotic, full from a week's worth of construction leftovers. I tied up Eddy-Spaghetti and Red Dog to the outdoor arena fence posts and turned Brenda Lee out to freely graze. Lucy (as usual) was free to be Lucy. I turned on the van stereo so I could listen to Rhonda Byrnes' (Author of *The Secret*), newest book *The Power*. I figured that maybe if I fed my mind a steady stream of love inspirations it would start to make me feel better.

I felt happy that Brenda Lee was going to get a good two hours of grazing on some lush fall grasses. I enjoyed the freedom of Lucy exploring the boundaries of our little family camp - but I still felt "blah".

I started emptying my van of all the equipment, junk and debris from a very productive week in remodeling and renovations. This meditative exercise of clearing and cleaning usually gives me some feeling of immediate gratification. While I felt satisfied that I was finally getting this done, the completion of it was less than the uplifting satisfaction I sought.

As I cleared and cleaned the clutter, I noticed Brenda Lee quietly grazing nearby. Lucy played, while Red Dog and Eddie Spaghetti sat quietly. They both seemed to have no desire to be anywhere else than here with our little group. This eased my mind that they were all at peace to be here with me while I finished sorting out the van clutter - but still, I felt "blah".

My well-being was only "just getting by". And I wanted more.

I started shifting my mind toward going to the gym for a leg workout, and I searched not only for the motivation I would need to do this, but I searched for desire itself.

I sat there quietly observing the peaceful community of my four-legged family - all of us relaxed and at peace together. I contemplated my lingering state of "blah", trying to move myself beyond it. As I did this, Brenda Lee made her way over to me and poked her massive head right into the van. She politely asked for carrots or apple treats (which I had) and I happily metered each one to her in order to prolong her stay in the van with her head in my lap. As she enjoyed each savory and crunchy bite, my soul was equally nourished by the much needed emotional nutrients her visit offered to me.

About this time, I was reminded by an alarm on my phone about a Skype session planned for twelve o'clock with Magali (the marketing manager for HKTWH) in Paris, France. Magali had set this time aside especially for me, so I had to attend -even though I had neither the motivation nor the desire to do so.

I packed up the peaceful moment, put Brenda Lee in her paddock and headed off to the coffee house near the gym to get WI-FI access.

As I sat in the van Skyping with Magali through many dropped connections, I realized I wasn't the least bit agitated at all of the disruptions. My calm was not result of a wise perspective, but more resulting from lack of feeling, I simply felt indifferent or apathetic about the extra time out Skype session was taking.

I thought, "Maybe it's my allergies affecting me so? Maybe it is my new sugar-free diet? ...maybe this, maybe that..." I didn't really even have the desire to look too hard for the answers, nor did I care to really delve into questioning this persistent state of "blah" any longer.

I talked with Magali about how proud I am of the whole team at HKTWH. We have accomplished so much over a short time with limited resources in a tough economy.
I also shared with her our commitment to excellence. We make sure we "walk our walk" as we help to guide others along their paths, as we pursue our own ways through the way of the horse.

I enjoyed hearing what I was saying. I really enjoyed feeling the truth behind each word. But there was still no spark. No movement. There was only the mundane maintenance of the status quo.

As I sat to write this whispering before going into the gym, I couldn't find the inspiration to come up with a "great" idea to write about that would be moving and satisfying for those who read this far. I decided to simply write about my day, tell my truth, and see if you can relate.

So, here I am before you, stuck in the state of "blah". What state have you gotten stuck in? How long were you stuck there? What finally moved you out of it?

As for me: No, I did not get a blinding bolt of the obvious. The skies did not open up to reveal anything particularly appealing as of yet, and the sun has not shined it's light into my grayness - as a matter of fact it has begun to drizzle.

However, a deep sense of awareness and gratitude has shown up to accompany my complacency.

An awareness of the fact that, no matter how I may feel, I have found a cause and have dedicated my life to pursuing it.
I am aware that this cause has attracted people whom I love creating with. An awareness that the vision, mission and plan for my life will carry me toward and forward - even when I want to lay down and take a nap!

I have an awareness that even on my "blah" days or my "gray" days, my "I don't care to care" days, that I have set in motion, by following my heart, a river of support that will support and carry me effortlessly even when I don't feel the desire to carry my own weight.

I recently watched a movie called "John Carter". At the end of the movie John was leaving this world behind to travel to a new life in new lands, and he gave this advice to his nephew who he was leaving his fortunes to:

1/. Find a cause 2/. Write a book 3/. Fall in love 4/. Go home.

I would only add "With your life" to the end of part 3. "Fall in love with your life" and even on those days when melancholy is all you can aspire to, you can smile deep inside while you float through the fog knowing that **you matter** - that **your life matters**.

Fall in love with your life! And even when you do trip and fall it will be for the only cause worth falling for: **Your Life!**

This is what I have found to be true.
(As a smile *finally* makes its way, unasked, to my cheeks.)

This is what I have found is working and playing for me.

Now... off to do that leg workout! (After I finish my coffee and enjoy this smile that is breaking through the gray!)

Maybe later today I will ask Brenda Lee to carry me through the forest as a passenger, full of gratitude for life's gift of awareness.

What is your cause? What is your "just because"? What is your story?
What do you love?

I hope you fall in love with your story - just because.

Ahhh! Now, that feels better. Thank you!

Feel the Connection

*"It is in the proper harnessing of our own
personal 'horsepower' that we can gain access to the energy that
creates our bliss."*

© Tina Thuell

BonusWhispering 2

Our Rented Planet, Your Gifted Time

*"You can't take any of this with you, so be grateful,
feeling the wonder of the gifts you are renting while you are here."
(Brenda Lee, HKTWH)*

Do you want to know "The secret", the key to unlocking life's treasures during your lifetime?

It is all OURS.
Now, get your brain to tell your feet to take you to the place and time to claim it.

If there is one thing that I have learned from Brenda Lee and Lucy, it is that we are linked in to everything, yet we don't own anything. I know this may seem a little paradoxical (maybe very paradoxical) but so be it.

Brenda Lee and Lucy see themselves as one part of everything. And in Lucy's case, in charge of everything!

When we realize that we are only here for a very short time compared to the time of things, or a very long time compared to the life of a flea, we can appreciate that we are only renters of this life experience. We can't take any of the material things we have created, collected, or attracted to us with us when we depart. It all stays here! So...what do you really own?

You own everything.
Your story of everything is how you experience it. And since you have control over your story, you have ownership over your relationship to the "Things" in this life, not to the things themselves.

"The secret" to unlocking your treasures is in realizing that you alone are responsible for everything in your life. And, that everything is ours.
When I'm walking with or riding on Brenda Lee, I'm acutely aware that I'm responsible for me - for my story. When I tell a connected, moving story she connects with me. When I tell my genuine, authentic, vulnerable truth to myself - she connects with me. When I don't - she doesn't! Plain and simple.

And when 1800 lbs of beautiful sentient being does not want to be with you it is glaringly obvious.
And when she does, it is heart-filling lovely.

Brenda Lee and Lucy want us to claim our right to our "OUR". When we accept that our life and the things that fill it are all OURS, then we accept full responsibility for the gratitude, grace, beauty and creative expression and expansion of it in a way that feels better in our hearts.

When you realize that it is all yours and ours, then you don't come from a place of lack. You come from a place of play, joy and the freedom of expression to what moves you.

IT was all here before you got here and it will all be here when you leave.

The important question is: "What will you add to IT with the time that you have left?"
Ask yourself: "If you could imagine that this is all ours and all yours, what do you want to do with it?"

Feel your connection to everything.
Choose the things that feel right to you.
Express your story of those things out loud for all to see.
Expand this place and time by the life you are living, utilizing everything that is... your OUR!

You don't' get to take any credit for what is - only for what you do with it.

So accept your "OUR" and tell your great story. Live a creative life and add *Yours* to *Ours*.

Brenda Lee and Lucy will enjoy connecting with that.

Feel the Connection

© Tina Thuell

© Tina Thuell

Photographs by

Jaimie & Jonathan Jusczyk

Jaimie Jusczyk, native Australian and living in the US, is a passionate photographer, videographer and web developer who joined the HKTWH team in 2010. She works behind the scenes with our team and is a one-of-a-kind highly skilled and creative multitask-monster.

Her innate love for horses, nature and animals in general makes her a wanted photographer for riders, equine facilities and any customized shoots. She creates your dreams from the first picture to video content, website or other products as calendars or albums.

Together with her husband, **Jonathan Jusczyk**, she films and edits the HKTWH workshop videos and the HKTWH Academy content.

Jaimie and Jonathan love capturing special moments and sharing them with you.

You can visit their website **www.AcuteShoot.com** to enjoy more of their work.

Tina Thuell

Tina Thuell is a fine art photographer with a passion for photographing horses. Born and raised in Bermuda, Tina currently lives in rural Pennsylvania with her husband Tim, their two dogs and the comings and goings of their 3 grown children.

While Tina enjoys many different aspects of photography, what brings her the greatest joy is photographing horses. *"It took a while for me to realize that I could take my love for photography and my lifelong passion for horses and bring them together. My 'Aha' moment came in 2005 after attending a workshop with renowned Equine photographer, Tony Stromberg. That was a critical turning point for me where I finally knew what I had to do. There is nothing like it, the absolute thrill of being surrounded by horses, especially out in the wilds, with camera in hand; it just does not get any better than that."*

Tina continues her education by traveling throughout the US and more recently through Europe, doing workshops and going on adventures with some of her favorite mentors and equine photographer friends. In addition she is a Professional member of The Equine Photographers Network.

Tina works strictly with Nikon Digital equipment. Not being technically minded, Tina tends to operate on an emotional level when photographing her subjects. *"For me one of the greatest joys of photography is in capturing the life and spirit of any given moment, be that in human nature or Mother Nature. A single photograph or a collection of photographs is considered by many to be priceless, a part of ones' history and something to be treasured for a lifetime and generations to come. Each time I can add to anyone's collection of treasures it brings me a great deal of Joy and I feel I have been successful".*

Please visit her website to see more of her work, book a private session or purchase a print.

www.TinaThuellPhotography.com

About Brian Reid and Horses Know The Way Home

Who is Brian Reid, Brenda Lee, Horses Know the Way Home - Feel the Connection?

That question is best answered and best understood by feeling for what is calling you toward.

As far back as Brian can remember he was looking for the reasons behind the reason of why things are the way they are. What is the energy that precedes the thoughts, feelings and actions we experience? What are our motivations? Where does our inspiration come from?

As a fitness director of health clubs, distributor and facilitator of personal development programs since the 80's, as a personal trainer, motivational speaker in the 90's, as creator of Inner Fitness Centers or lecturer on fitness and motivation at the United States Navy's Elite schools, Brian has always sought to put himself in a position to discover *what moves people*. He has always been passionate about how to apply his discoveries in his life and teach others to feel their connection to their own "flow".

He has applied these movement creation skills in his own life in recovering from life robbing addictions; taking his residential remodeling business from a man with a circular saw to being recognized as one of the top 50 companies in the industry in the US in only 6 years; going from 280 lbs and not having worked out in 8 years to winning the novice Mr. America in 17 months with 1% body fat.

The ability to move our lives toward our dreams in a timeframe indefinable by the story of our past experiences, is what Brian has thrown himself into and committed his life to sharing.

That we are all already enough and the creation of that story, the expressing of our desires that the living of our life has inspired, is what Brian is committed to.

While walking this path, Brian happened upon a beautiful 1 year old Shire mare named Brenda Lee. It was through this relationship and partnership that Brian experienced the truth of the flow, the go and the movement that is the natural expression of who we are that lovingly calls us home.

The secrets that Brenda Lee unveiled to Brian during their extensive personal and private time in the forests and seaside beaches of southern New England during the first 8 years of Brenda Lee's life, were the prerequisites to the creation of Horses Know the Way Home. It was during the "Just Sit There" time, doing nothing, asking nothing, expecting nothing that everything started to peek through. Brenda Lee's size, power, beauty and accepting awareness created the nurturing space for nature's secrets to flourish into practical, applicable, natural facts.

During this time Brian was having internal conversations about what was at the core of what horses were offering humans. It was more than carrying our body weight; it was carrying our love toward home, toward the alignment of our highest and best selves.

Horses Know the Way Home- Feel the Connection is the combination of a lifetime of training skills to help humans move toward the natural expression of their beautiful next, to move from *being* to their best felt *becoming*.

Brian would like you to experience the facts of the horse to help you live the aligned, flowing, inspired metaphor of your life and create a great story.
The horse is the essence of what human words are pointing toward. When we say "Be here now", "Be Present", "Be Aware", "To be or not to be", "To thine own self be true", we are describing a way of being that the horses are actually becoming, they are the living verbs of those ideals.

In bringing understanding, clarity and connection to the actual energy and vibration that moves us to new places, spaces, possibilities and potential, Brian lives to facilitate, support, accelerate and amplify "movement toward what matters."

Brian's dream is that you will feel the connection to that which connects us all and "Let Go" so you can move Toward your "Let's Go". To find and feel your "Yesses" and live your life toward your Best Yes yet.

The expression of this dream is the essence, the mission and the vision of Horses Know The Way Home.

Your life is calling you home, answer the call!

More information:

www.HorsesKnowTheWayHome.com